The Communication Compass

Guiding Lights for Building Rapport, Trust, and Fulfilling Connections

Andrea Berry

Copyright

©2024 Andrea Berry

The Communication Compass

Table of Contents

Introduction

Chapter One
Foundations of Self-Awareness - Unraveling the Bedrock for Meaningful Communication

Chapter Two
Initiating Conversations with Finesse - Practical Tips and Anecdotes Demystifying the Art of Starting Dialogues

Chapter Three
The Silent Symphony of Body Language - Harnessing the Power of Gestures, Expressions, and Posture

Chapter Four
Engaging Small Talk as Bridges to Understanding - Unveiling the Secrets of Transformative, Meaningful Exchanges

Chapter Five
Building a Solid Framework for Rapport - Foundations of Good Communication Laid Bare

Chapter Six
Navigating the Profound Waters of Connection - Unlocking the Potential for Richer, More Fulfilling Relationships

Chapter Seven
Tools for Stormy Seas: Navigating Difficult Personalities - Turning Discord into Opportunities for Growth

Chapter Eight
Companion on the Journey - Beyond a Guide: Your Companion to Becoming a Masterful Communicator

Conclusion

Introduction

Within the fast-paced embroidered artwork of life, where connections weave the texture of our presence, acing the craftsmanship of communication becomes important. I'm Andrea Berry, a tenacious relationship expert with an enthusiasm for unraveling the complexities that regularly tangle our associations with others. Through a long time of committed work in family, social, and commerce domains, I've experienced the obstacles that communication can present.

This journey hasn't been without its challenges, but from these challenges, I've refined a set of principles that frame the spine of compelling communication. This book is my endeavour to share these principles with you, offering bits of knowledge and methodologies to explore the assorted scenes of human interaction.

At the heart of these standards may be a significant understanding of oneself—the bedrock upon which all significant communication is built. From this self-awareness springs the capacity to start discussions with artfulness, a skill I delve into with down-to-earth tips and accounts that demystify the craftsmanship of beginning important conversations.

But communication extends beyond words—it's a dance of body language, a silent ensemble that talks volumes. Unpacking the subtleties of non-verbal signals, I direct you to tackle the control of your gestures, expressions and poses to amplify the reverberation of your message.

Small talk, frequently dismissed as trivial, is the portal to more deeper associations. I disentangle the privileged insights of locks in small talk, changing ordinary exchanges into bridges that span the profundities of understanding. The establishments of great communication are uncovered, leaving you with a strong framework to build trust and rapport.

However, the quintessence of communication lies not in the surface but within the depths of significant exchanges. I guide you in exploring these significant waters, opening the potential for wealthier, more satisfying associations. When confronted with the challenges of difficult personalities, I equip you with tools to explore those stormy oceans, turning friction into an opportunity for development.

This book is more than a guide; it's a companion on your journey to getting to be an unbelievable communicator. Whether you look for harmony in your family, victory in your career, or genuine connections in your social circles, these principles will be your compass.

Embark with me on this exploration of the craftsmanship and science of communication. Let's disentangle the strings that tie us and weave a tapestry of connections that withstand the test of time. Welcome to a transformative journey—one discussion at a time.

Chapter One

Foundations of Self-Awareness - Unraveling the Bedrock for Meaningful Communication

In the vast tapestry of human experience, self-awareness stands as the foundational thread, weaving intricate patterns that shape the contours of our lives. This chapter embarks on a journey into the depths of self-awareness, exploring its significance as the bedrock of meaningful communication.

The Essence of Self-Awareness
Self-awareness, the conscious knowledge of one's character, feelings, motives, and desires, is the cornerstone of personal development. It reflects the complexities of our inner selves, providing a roadmap to navigate the labyrinth of emotions, thoughts, and actions. Without this fundamental understanding, effective communication remains elusive, as it relies on articulating one's thoughts and feelings. Self-awareness is not a static state but a dynamic process of peeling away the layers that shroud our authentic selves. We delve into the intricacies of unraveling these layers, encouraging readers to explore the depths of their consciousness.

- Unraveling the Layers: Exploring the Depths of Consciousness

Practical Tips
• Journaling Practices: Maintain a journal for self-reflection. Writing thoughts, feelings, and experiences can unveil layers of consciousness and provide insights into personal growth.

• Mindfulness Techniques: Mindfulness exercises help you to stay present and attuned to your thoughts and emotions. Mindful breathing, meditation, or body scans facilitate the unraveling process.

• Questioning Assumptions: Question assumptions and beliefs about yourself. Challenging preconceived notions may uncover hidden layers that could have been shaped by external influences.

• Exploring Personal Narratives: Explore personal narratives and life stories. Analysing pivotal moments and their impact on personal growth can reveal layers of consciousness that may have been overlooked.

Layers of Consciousness:
1. Surface Level: The outermost layer represents the surface level, where societal expectations, roles, and immediate responses reside. Recognize and understand these external influences on your identity.

2. Emotional Depths: Beneath the surface, emotions form a layer that often influences reactions and decisions. Understand and embrace emotions as integral components of self-awareness.

3. Core Values and Beliefs: Unraveling deeper involves identifying and examining core values and beliefs. This layer shapes the fundamental principles guiding one's actions and choices.

4. Unconscious Patterns: Delve into the unconscious mind to uncover patterns, habits, and behaviours that operate beneath awareness. When you bring these patterns to light, you gain an understanding of your automatic responses.

Scenario:
Emma experiences stress in professional settings. By unraveling the layers, Emma discovered that this stress was rooted in childhood experiences of pressure to succeed. This exploration allowed Emma to address the underlying cause and develop strategies for managing stress in a more informed way.

Empowering Self-Discovery:

This section aims to empower readers to embark on a journey of self-discovery, peeling back the layers of consciousness with courage and curiosity. By unraveling these layers, individuals gain an understanding of their authentic selves, fostering a profound connection with their thoughts, emotions, and aspirations. This exploration sets the stage for enhanced self-awareness and more meaningful interactions with the world.

By understanding the core aspects of their identity, readers can cultivate a genuine connection with themselves, laying the groundwork for authentic communication.

- Mirror of Reflection
Communication is a dance between minds, an intricate interplay of words, gestures, and expressions. To engage in meaningful communication with others, one must first be in tune with themselves. Self-awareness is a mirror of reflection, allowing individuals to comprehend their biases, fears, and aspirations. With this introspective lens, readers can navigate the subtle currents of interpersonal dynamics with clarity and empathy.

- The Intersection of Language and Emotion
Language is the bridge that spans the chasm between minds, but its efficacy is linked with

emotional intelligence. We explore the symbiotic relationship between language and emotion, emphasizing how self-awareness is the compass for navigating this intricate terrain.

Understanding the Symbiosis:
Language is the medium through which emotions are expressed, and emotions, in turn, shape the nuances and depth of language. This symbiosis is a dynamic interplay that influences how individuals communicate and connect with others.

Practical Tips for Navigating Language and Emotion:
• Reflect on your emotional vocabulary. Deep and expansive emotional vocabulary enhances the ability to articulate feelings accurately.

• Engage in the practice of journaling as a tool for emotional expression. With writing, individuals can explore and articulate their emotions, fostering a deeper understanding of their inner world.

• Learn the need for mindful communication practices, emphasizing the importance of being present in conversations. Conscious listening and thoughtful expression contribute to a more harmonious interplay between language and emotion.

• Recognizing the significance of non-verbal cues in communication. Being self-aware enables individuals to recognize and interpret these cues, adding layers of meaning to verbal expressions.

Scenario:
Consider Jane, who, during a team meeting, notices a colleague's subtle expressions of frustration. By being self-aware, Jane recognizes the emotional undercurrent and adjusts her communication approach. Instead of dismissing the frustration, she addresses it empathetically, fostering a more open and effective dialogue.

Navigating the Intricacies:
• Expressive Language: Self-awareness empowers individuals to use language for expressing complex emotions. By acknowledging and understanding their emotional state, individuals can express their feelings more clearly, fostering mutual understanding in conversations.

• Empathetic Communication: Being in tune with one's emotions allows individuals to recognize and validate the feelings of others, creating a space for compassionate and meaningful interactions.

• Navigating Emotional Challenges: When faced with emotionally charged situations, self-awareness becomes the compass guiding individuals through the terrain of language and emotion. It aids in choosing thoughtful words, avoiding escalation, and promoting constructive dialogue.

• Cultivating Emotional Intelligence: Self-awareness is integral to cultivating emotional intelligence. This, in turn, enhances one's ability to navigate the subtleties of language and emotion, fostering healthier and more authentic connections with others.

- Breaking the Barriers
Meaningful communication often encounters barriers – preconceived notions, biases, and unspoken assumptions. The journey into self-awareness outlined in this chapter is a transformative process that dismantles these barriers. By shedding light on the unconscious elements that influence communication, individuals can foster a more inclusive and open dialogue, transcending the limitations placed by unexamined perspectives.

- The Power of Vulnerability
At the heart of self-awareness lies the courage to embrace vulnerability. Through acknowledging and expressing vulnerability, individuals form deeper

connections, as authenticity becomes the catalyst for genuine understanding and empathy.

- Mindful Presence
Communication transcends the spoken word; it is an exchange that encompasses presence and mindfulness. There is a need to be fully present in interactions. From mindful presence, individuals can discern the unspoken cues, fostering a connection that extends beyond verbal exchanges.

- Nurturing Emotional Resilience
Effective communication requires emotional resilience – the ability to wade through the highs and lows of interpersonal interactions. Through acknowledging and understanding emotional triggers, individuals can respond to challenges with grace and resilience, contributing to a communicative environment that fosters growth and understanding.

Chapter One has laid the groundwork for a transformative exploration into the depths of the self. By unraveling the layers of consciousness, readers embark on a journey that enhances their self-awareness and serves as the cornerstone for meaningful communication. Through introspection, vulnerability, and mindfulness, individuals can navigate the intricate landscape of human connection, fostering a communicative environment that is authentic, empathetic, and transformative.

Chapter Two

Initiating Conversations with Finesse - Practical Tips and Anecdotes Demystifying the Art of Starting Dialogues

The Prelude to Connection

Initiating a conversation is the prelude to forging connections, a delicate dance that requires finesse and understanding. Here, we delve into the art of starting dialogues, offering practical tips and relatable anecdotes to demystify the process. From casual encounters to formal settings, the ability to initiate conversations with finesse is a skill that transcends social boundaries, fostering meaningful connections.

Reading the Room

The first step in initiating conversations with finesse is to read the room. We explore the nuances of assessing the social environment, understanding the energy, and gauging the receptiveness of those present.

1. Navigating Social Dynamics: Assessing Environment, Energy, and Receptiveness

Assessing the Social Environment:

Understanding the social environment involves perceiving the context and dynamics of a given situation. It's about taking stock of the physical setting, the people present, and the overall atmosphere. For instance, entering a corporate networking event may have a formal ambiance, while a casual gathering with friends may be more relaxed. There is a need to assess the environment to tailor your approach, ensuring it aligns with the specific social context.

Tips:
- Observe Decor and Setting: Take note of the venue's decor, layout, and overall aesthetics. These offer clues about the formality or informality of the setting.
- Note Group Dynamics: Identify existing groups and notice their interactions. This insight helps in gauging the existing social structure and finding entry points for conversation.

Understanding the Energy:
The energy within a social setting is the collective mood, vibe, and emotional tone. It involves tuning into the prevailing emotions, whether lively, subdued, or somewhere in between. By understanding the energy, individuals can align their behaviour to match

the atmosphere, contributing positively to the overall dynamics of the gathering.

Tips:
- Observe Body Language: Pay attention to the body language of individuals. Are people animated and expressive, or more reserved? Body language can provide valuable cues about the overall energy of the environment.
- Listen to Conversational Tones: The tone of conversations, including volume and intensity, can reflect the energy of the setting. Adapt your conversational style to complement the prevailing atmosphere.

Gauging Receptiveness:
Assessing receptiveness involves understanding how open and welcoming the individuals in the social setting are to engagement. This skill allows you to gauge whether it's an opportune time to initiate conversations or if a more observant approach is needed. It's about recognizing cues that signal receptiveness or potential barriers.

Tips:
- Eye Contact and Smiles: Friendly eye contact and smiles are positive indicators of receptiveness. If

these cues are in place, it's likely a time to initiate a conversation.
- Open Body Language: Look for signs of open body language, such as uncrossed arms and facing towards the group. These signals suggest a more welcoming environment.
- Engagement in Conversations: Observe if people are engaged in ongoing conversations. If conversations are moving smoothly, it might be a conducive time to join in.

Scenario:
Imagine walking into a social gathering and observing a group engaged in lively conversations with open body language and frequent smiles. The energy in the room is vibrant. These cues suggest receptiveness, prompting you to approach the group and seamlessly become part of the ongoing conversation.

2. The Icebreaker Arsenal

Icebreakers are the unsung heroes of conversation initiation. We introduce a diverse arsenal of icebreaker techniques, from light-hearted jokes to thought-provoking questions. By providing you with a toolbox of engaging icebreakers, we aim to empower individuals to navigate the initial moments of a conversation with confidence and ease, setting the stage for deeper engagement.

Diverse Icebreaker Techniques:
• Light-Hearted Jokes:
   - Start with a classic icebreaker joke. For example: "Why did the scarecrow win an award? Because he was outstanding in his field!" Light-hearted humour can instantly create a positive atmosphere and set the tone for a friendly conversation.

• The Compliment Game:
   - Offer a genuine compliment to initiate a conversation. Whether it's about someone's attire, a project they worked on, or their positive energy, compliments are a delightful way to break the ice and make the other person feel appreciated.

• Two Truths and a Lie:
   - Share one false statement and two true ones about yourself. Encourage the other person to guess which statement is the lie. This game adds an element of intrigue and encourages a playful exchange of personal anecdotes.

• The Thought-Provoking Question:
   - Pose a question that sparks contemplation, such as "If you could have dinner with any historical figure, who would it be and why?" Thought-provoking

questions encourage deeper discussion and reveal parts of a person's personality.

- Name Association Game:
  - Associate the person's name with a positive attribute or a fun memory. For instance, "Every time I hear your name, I think of adventure!" This adds a personal touch and infuses the interaction with positivity.

- The Quirky Fact Swap:
  - Share a quirky or interesting fact about yourself, and encourage the other party to do the same. This light-hearted exchange of unique titbits creates an instant connection and often leads to laughter.

- Memory Lane:
  - Reminisce about a shared experience or event, even a simple memory like a team-building activity or a past encounter. This icebreaker technique builds on shared history, creating a sense of camaraderie.

- The Movie Buff Question:
  - Ask about their favourite movie or TV show and why it resonates with them. It opens the door to discussing shared interests and provides insights into their personality and preferences.

- The Future Aspiration Inquiry:

- Inquire about the person's future aspirations or goals. For example, "What's one thing you've always wanted to achieve, and how are you working towards it?" This icebreaker encourages a forward-looking and optimistic conversation.

• The Pet Story Exchange:
  - Share a funny or heartwarming story about a pet, and invite the other person to do the same. Pet stories often evoke positive emotions and create a light-hearted atmosphere for conversation.

• The Book Recommendation:
  - Ask for a book recommendation or share a recent favourite. This icebreaker reveals literary preferences and leads to discussions about broader topics, fostering intellectual engagement.

By having a diverse arsenal of icebreaker techniques, you can adapt your approach based on the context and preferences of the individuals involved, making conversation initiation a dynamic and enjoyable experience.

3. Authenticity in Approach

Authenticity forms the bedrock of meaningful connections. We emphasize the importance of genuine and authentic approaches in conversation initiation.

- Expanding on the Statement:
The essence of authentic conversation initiation lies in the genuine expression of oneself. It involves embracing one's true identity, thoughts, and emotions, allowing for a natural and sincere connection with others. By steering clear of artificiality, individuals create an environment where authenticity becomes the catalyst for building meaningful and genuine connections.

Scenario:
Joan attends a networking event of polished professionals engaging in rehearsed elevator pitches. Feeling out of place, she decides to be herself. Instead of delivering a standard introduction, she shares a personal story about her journey in the industry, including both triumphs and challenges. This authenticity sets her apart and attracts individuals who appreciate her genuine approach, leading to more meaningful conversations and potential collaborations.

Tips:
• Share Personal Narratives:
   - Instead of depending on generic introductions, share personal narratives that reflect your experiences, values, and passions. It provides a

glimpse into your authentic self and encourages others to reciprocate with their own stories.

• Express Vulnerability:
   - Don't be afraid to express vulnerability in your conversations. Share moments of struggle, growth, or uncertainty. Authenticity often blossoms in moments of vulnerability, creating a space for others to connect on a deeper level.

• Be Present in the Moment:
   - Practice being fully present during conversations. Put away distractions and focus on the person you are engaging with. Authenticity flourishes when individuals feel genuinely heard and acknowledged.

• Listen Actively:
   - Authenticity is a two-way street. Actively listen to others, validating their experiences and opinions. It fosters an environment where everyone feels valued, contributing to the authenticity of the interaction.

• Stay True to Your Values:
   - In conversation initiation, stay true to your values. Avoid conforming to societal expectations or adopting personas that don't align with who you are. Authentic

connections thrive when individuals are genuine to themselves.

- Use Natural Language:
  - Avoid overly formal or rehearsed language. Using natural language contributes to a relaxed atmosphere, making it easier for authenticity to shine through.

- Celebrate being unique:
  - Embrace and celebrate your uniqueness. Instead of trying to fit into a mold, highlight what makes you different. Authentic connections often stem from appreciating and understanding the diverse qualities that each individual brings to the conversation.

- Learn from Mistakes:
  - Authenticity doesn't mean perfection. If you make a mistake or say something that feels off, acknowledge it. Learning from these moments and being open about them contributes to a sense of realness and fosters trust.

- Avoid Overthinking:
  - Authenticity thrives in spontaneity. Avoid overthinking your words or actions. Let the conversation flow naturally. Overthinking can lead to artificiality, hindering the development of genuine connections.

- Follow Up with Genuine Interest:
    - After initiating a conversation, follow up with genuine interest. Ask about the other person's experiences, thoughts, or interests. Demonstrating ongoing curiosity and investment in the connection reinforces authenticity.

4. The Power of Observation

Initiating conversations with finesse requires a keen sense of observation. We explore how the power of observation can be used to find common ground, identify shared interests, and create a natural flow in conversations. By honing this skill, individuals can connect with others on a deeper level, transcending surface-level exchanges to build more meaningful relationships.

Harnessing the Power of Observation in Conversation:

Observation is a powerful tool that can significantly enhance the quality of conversations. By keenly observing the details of the environment and the individuals involved, one can identify common ground, pinpoint shared interests, and facilitate a natural flow in conversations.

Key Components:

• Environmental Awareness:
   - The first step in harnessing observation is being aware of your surroundings. Take note of the setting, ambiance, and the people present. Are you in a formal or casual environment? Is there a specific theme or mood?

• Non-Verbal Cues:
   - Pay attention to facial expressions, gestures and body language. These cues provide valuable insights into the emotions and comfort levels of those around you. Subtle nods, smiles, or frowns can guide you in understanding the dynamics of the conversation.

• Listening Beyond Words:
   - Observation extends to active listening. Beyond the spoken words, observe the tone, pitch, and emphasis in someone's speech. It can convey emotions and nuances that are not explicitly stated.

• Identifying Commonalities:
   - Use observation to identify commonalities between yourself and others. Notice shared experiences, interests, or values. For example, if you

observe someone reading a book you enjoyed, it becomes a potential topic to initiate a conversation.

• Adapting to Group Dynamics:
   - In group settings, observe the dynamics between individuals. Note who seems more extroverted, who may be quieter but engaged, and how people naturally interact with each other. This awareness helps in gauging the rhythm of the conversation.

• Seizing Opportune Moments:
   - Timing is crucial in conversation. Observation allows you to identify opportune moments to contribute to the discussion or introduce a new topic. For instance, if someone expresses enthusiasm about a subject, it may be the perfect time to share a related experience or idea.

• Creating a Comfortable Environment:
   - Observation can guide you in creating a comfortable environment for conversation. Adjust your approach based on the observed comfort levels of those involved. Being attuned to non-verbal cues helps the conversation flow naturally without causing discomfort.

Scenario:

Imagine you're attending a networking event, and you observe a group discussing recent industry trends. Instead of jumping into the conversation with generic remarks, your observational skills prompt you to notice someone holding a cup of coffee with a logo from a well-known tech company. This observation becomes a key to finding common ground. You approach the person and initiate a conversation about the latest innovations in the tech industry, seamlessly connecting over shared professional interests.

Tips:
• Practice Mindful Presence:
   - Be fully present in the moment, engaging your senses to absorb information from your surroundings. This mindfulness enhances your observational abilities.

• Ask Open-Ended Questions:
   - Use observations to formulate open-ended questions that invite deep responses.

• Cultivate Curiosity:
   - Approach conversations with genuine curiosity. The more you observe and inquire, the more likely you will discover common ground and shared interests.

- Continuous Improvement:
  - Reflect on your observations after conversations. What did you notice that worked well? What could be improved? Use these reflections to refine your observational skills.

By actively harnessing the power of observation, individuals can uncover shared interests, find common ground, and naturally guide conversations toward more authentic and enriching exchanges.

5. Non-verbal Communication

Words are only a fraction of the conversation. Non-verbal cues play a significant role in the art of initiation. From body language to eye contact, these are subtle signals that invite or discourage interaction. Readers gain insights into harnessing the power of non-verbal communication, allowing them to convey openness and approachability in their initiation efforts.

6. Overcoming Introversion

Initiating conversations can be particularly challenging for introverted individuals.
Unique struggles experienced by introverts include social exhaustion, difficulty initiating conversations, and feeling overlooked. Strategies to overcome these struggles include setting social boundaries, using

icebreakers, and finding quieter spaces for recharge. By embracing introversion as a strength and leveraging personalized approaches, introverted readers can initiate conversations with finesse, navigating social interactions with authenticity and confidence.

7. Contextual Relevance

Not all conversations are created equal, and the art of finesse lies in recognizing the relevance of the conversation within a given context. To align conversation initiation with the environment
- observe surroundings and consider shared interests.
- Choose topics related to the setting or events, ensuring relevance.
- Gauge the mood and adapt your conversation to suit the individuals present, fostering a more engaging and resonant interaction.

By understanding the importance of context, readers can tailor their approach for maximum impact.

8. Navigating Cultural Sensitivities

In an interconnected world, conversations often transcend cultural boundaries. Navigating cultural sensitivities is a crucial aspect of initiating conversations with finesse. Understand cultural nuances by educating yourself on diverse customs, norms, and communication styles. Respect personal boundaries and avoid assumptions. Initiate conversations with neutral topics, listen actively, and be open-minded. Adapt your communication style to be inclusive and foster a respectful exchange of ideas. By embracing cultural awareness, individuals can foster connections that transcend geographical and cultural differences.

9. Embrace Vulnerability

Vulnerability is a powerful catalyst for connection. Embrace vulnerability in conversation initiation by sharing personal stories and experiences. Through relatable anecdotes, readers learn how vulnerability can create an environment of trust and authenticity, paving the way for more profound and meaningful connections.

Learning from Anecdotes
- The Coffee Shop Connection
John, a self-professed introvert, challenges himself by striking up conversations with strangers in his local coffee shop. He noticed a person reading a book he had recently enjoyed and mustered the courage to pay compliment their choice. This small icebreaker led to a delightful conversation about shared literary interests, turning a casual encounter into a newfound friendship that extended beyond the confines of the coffee shop.

- Navigating Cross-Cultural Conversations
Maria, a travel enthusiast, found herself at a multicultural gathering where conversation initiation seemed like threading a cultural minefield. Unsure of where to start, she shared a humorous anecdote about cultural misunderstandings from her travels. This light-hearted approach diffused tension and opened the floodgates for others to share their cross-cultural experiences, turning a potentially awkward situation into a celebration of diversity.

- The Power of Vulnerability at a Networking Event
At a networking event, Jimm noticed the familiar sea of professionals exchanging business cards and pleasantries. Instead of sticking to the usual industry talk, he shared a personal struggle he had experienced in his career. To his surprise, this vulnerability resonated with others, leading to more genuine and meaningful conversations. The event transformed from a transactional exchange to a space where professionals could connect on a human level.

- The Unexpected Connection on Public Transportation
During a long bus ride, Carmen saw herself sitting next to someone absorbed in a book she had read

recently. Instead of staying silent, she mustered the courage to strike up a conversation about the book. To their mutual surprise, they discovered a shared passion for the author's work, turning a mundane commute into a delightful exchange that extended beyond the bus ride.

These relatable anecdotes showcase the diverse scenarios in which individuals can initiate conversations with finesse. Whether in professional settings, coffee shops, multicultural gatherings, networking events, or public transportation, the art of conversation initiation has the potential to turn everyday encounters into meaningful connections.

10. Practice Makes Proficiency

Initiating conversations is a skill that is honed through practice. Below are actionable exercises to enhance your conversation initiation skills. From simulated scenarios to reflective exercises, you are encouraged to actively engage in the learning process, building the confidence and proficiency needed to initiate conversations with finesse in various settings.

Exercises to Enhance Conversation Initiation Skills:
- The Daily Icebreaker Challenge:
    - Commit to starting a conversation with a new person every day for a week. Focus on using different icebreakers, from simple compliments to

thought-provoking questions. Reflect on the experiences and note any patterns in the responses you receive.

• Contextual Observation Journal:
   - Carry a small notebook and jot down observations about the social environments you find yourself in. Note the energy, mood, and dynamics of the space. Challenge yourself to initiate a conversation that aligns with the observed context. Over time, this practice hones your ability to read and adapt to various social settings.

• Cultural Exchange Evening:
   - Host a small gathering with friends from diverse cultural backgrounds. Each person can share a cultural anecdote or tradition, creating an environment that encourages open dialogue. Practice initiating conversations by asking questions about each other's backgrounds, fostering a rich exchange of experiences.

• The Vulnerability Journal:
   - Set aside time each week to reflect on personal experiences, challenges, or successes. Practice articulating these moments in a way that is open and vulnerable. Share your reflections with a trusted friend or mentor. This exercise enhances your

storytelling abilities and prepares you to initiate conversations with authenticity.

• Random Topic Generator:
  - Create a list of diverse and interesting conversation topics. Use a random topic generator or pick one from your list daily. Challenge yourself to initiate a conversation with someone new based on the chosen topic. This exercise expands your conversational repertoire and encourages adaptability.

• Silent Observation Exercise:
  - Attend a public space, such as a park or café, and silently observe people around you. Without engaging in conversation, practice interpreting non-verbal cues and body language. This exercise sharpens your observational skills, making you more attuned to the dynamics of social situations.

• Networking Role-Play:
  - Enlist a friend or mentor to engage in networking role-play scenarios. Practice initiating conversations in professional settings, navigating introductions, and seamlessly transitioning between topics. Receive constructive feedback to refine your approach and build confidence in networking environments.

- Story Swap Circle:
   - Gather a group of friends or colleagues for a storytelling circle. Each person takes turns sharing a short, personal story. The listener then initiates a conversation related to the shared story. This exercise enhances both storytelling and conversation initiation skills in a supportive setting.

- Cross-Cultural Coffee Meetup:
   - Arrange a casual coffee meetup with friends from different cultural backgrounds. Share anecdotes or traditions unique to your cultures and engage in conversations exploring the diversity within the group. This exercise fosters cultural awareness and provides opportunities to initiate meaningful discussions.

- Reflection and Adaptation Journal:
   - Maintain a journal where you reflect on your conversation initiation experiences. Note what worked well, what could be improved, and any insights gained. Use this journal to adapt your approach, experiment with different strategies, and track your progress over time.

By incorporating these actionable exercises into your routine, you actively engage in the process of enhancing your conversation initiation skills.

Remember, like any skill, proficiency comes with practice and a willingness to step outside your comfort zone.

In concluding this exploration into the art of initiating conversations with finesse, it becomes evident that this skill is not just a means to an end but a lifelong asset. The ability to connect with others through thoughtful conversation initiation transcends professional and personal spheres. It enriches the tapestry of human experience, fostering relationships built on genuine understanding, empathy, and shared moments.

By embracing the tips, anecdotes, and exercises presented in this chapter, readers embark on a journey to master the art of starting dialogues. Whether in a crowded room or a one-on-one setting, the finesse of conversation initiation becomes a beacon that illuminates the path to meaningful connections. Through observation, authenticity, cultural awareness, and the power of vulnerability, individuals can navigate the intricate dance of conversation initiation with grace, creating bridges that span the diverse landscapes of human interaction.

Chapter Three

The Silent Symphony of Body Language - Harnessing the Power of Gestures, Expressions, and Posture

We delve into the intricate world of facial expressions, exploring how our faces become the canvas of unspoken emotions. The silent symphony of body language finds its crescendo in the nuances of gestures, expressions, and posture. Understanding this dance unlocks a profound ability to connect, communicate, and interpret the unspoken language that permeates our daily interactions.

The Facial Canvas
Facial expressions serve as a captivating and intricate palette within the realm of non-verbal communication, acting as a primary means to convey emotions, thoughts, and intentions without uttering a single word. The human face, equipped with muscles, becomes a canvas upon which the silent symphony of emotions is painted.

• Universal Language:
  - Across cultures and languages, certain facial expressions are universally recognized. Joy, sadness, anger, surprise, fear, and disgust are basic

emotions identified by everyone. This universality highlights the primal nature of facial expressions as a fundamental means of human connection.

• Nuances and Variations:
   - While basic emotions are shared, the nuances and intensity of facial expressions can vary. Cultural, social, and individual factors contribute to subtle differences in how emotions are expressed. Understanding these variations enhances our ability to interpret the depth and context of someone's emotional state.

• Mirror Neurons and Empathy:
   - The phenomenon of mirror neurons plays a crucial role in our ability to connect through facial expressions. When we observe someone's facial expression, mirror neurons in our brains simulate that expression, fostering empathy and emotional resonance. This neurological mechanism is fundamental to the human capacity for understanding and sharing emotions.

• Micro expressions:
   - Facial expressions go beyond the overt display of emotions. Micro expressions, brief and involuntary facial movements lasting only a fraction of a second, provide glimpses into authentic emotional reactions.

Recognizing these subtle cues allows individuals to grasp underlying feelings not explicitly communicated.

- Cultural Influences:
  - Cultural context significantly shapes facial expressions. Certain cultures may encourage or discourage the overt display of emotions. Awareness of cultural nuances helps prevent misinterpretation and ensures effective cross-cultural communication. For instance, a smile may convey happiness in one culture but politeness or nervousness in another.

- Social Signalling:
  - Facial expressions act as social signals, facilitating communication in social settings. Raised eyebrows indicate surprise or interest, while a furrowed brow may suggest confusion or concern. The interplay of eye contact, smiles, and frowns creates a dynamic language that enhances interpersonal understanding.

- Emotional Regulation:
  - Individuals often use facial expressions to regulate and control their emotional expressions consciously or unconsciously. Understanding how people manage their facial expressions provides insights into their emotional state and self-regulation strategies.

Facial expressions are a fascinating blend of universal elements shared across humanity and culturally specific nuances that add complexity to the silent language of emotions.

Universal Aspects of Facial Expressions

• Basic Emotions:
  - Research, such as that by Paul Ekman, has identified a set of basic emotions—joy, sadness, anger, surprise, fear, and disgust—universally expressed through facial expressions. These expressions transcend cultural boundaries, suggesting a common biological and evolutionary foundation for human emotions.

• Facial Action Coding System (FACS):
  - The Facial Action Coding System, developed by Ekman and Wallace V. Friesen, breaks down facial expressions into specific muscle movements, creating a standardized way to describe and analyze facial behaviours. This system highlights the universal nature of facial actions associated with different emotions.

• Mirror Neurons and Emotional Contagion:
  - Mirror neurons, neural cells that fire when an individual performs an action and observes the same

action in another, contribute to the contagious nature of emotions. Seeing facial expressions associated with specific emotions triggers mirror neurons, fostering emotional contagion and shared experiences across diverse cultures.

Culturally Specific Aspects:
• Display Rules:
   - While basic emotions are expressed universally, cultures often dictate display rules—norms governing when, where, and how emotions are displayed. For example, some cultures may encourage the open expression of joy, while others prioritize emotional restraint, influencing how individuals manifest their feelings.

• Masking and Amplification:
   - Cultural norms can shape the way individuals mask or amplify their emotions. Some cultures value emotional restraint, leading individuals to suppress facial expressions, while others may encourage more expressive displays. Understanding these variations prevents misinterpretation of emotional states.

• Contextual Interpretation:
   - The interpretation of facial expressions is heavily influenced by cultural context. A smile, for instance, may signify happiness, politeness, or nervousness depending on cultural norms. Awareness of these

variations is crucial for accurate cross-cultural communication and avoiding misunderstandings.

• Emphasis on Different Expressions:
   - Cultures may prioritize and emphasize certain emotions over others. For instance, a culture that values collectivism might place a higher emphasis on expressions conveying harmony and group cohesion, while individualistic cultures may emphasize expressions of personal achievement and autonomy.

• Emotional Valence:
   - The perceived positivity or negativity of emotions can vary across cultures. What one culture views as a positive and acceptable display of enthusiasm may be seen as excessive or inappropriate in another. Understanding the cultural valence of emotions helps navigate social interactions effectively.

While universal elements lay the foundation for facial expressions, the cultural overlay adds depth and diversity to the silent symphony of emotions. Navigating these universal and culturally specific aspects enriches our ability to interpret and respond to the complex tapestry of human expressions in a globalized and interconnected world.

Micro expressions

Micro expressions are involuntary and short facial movements lasting less than a second. They offer a fascinating peep into an individual's emotional state. Often occurring spontaneously, these micro expressions are not easy to control and they provide a window into real feelings that are not openly expressed.

• The Subtlety of Micro expressions:
   - Micro expressions are subtle and are challenging to detect, as they occur rapidly and often go unnoticed in regular social interactions. However, their fleeting nature doesn't diminish their significance; they are authentic and can reveal emotions that a person might be trying to conceal.

• Paul Ekman's Research:
   - Psychologist Paul Ekman extensively researched micro expressions and incorporated them into his work on facial expressions. He identified seven universal micro expressions associated with basic emotions: happiness, sadness, fear, surprise, anger, disgust, and contempt. Recognizing these micro expressions contributes to a more nuanced understanding of underlying emotions.

• Involuntary Nature:
   - Unlike intentional facial expressions, micro expressions are involuntary, originating from the

limbic system—the emotional part of the brain. This involuntary aspect makes them a reliable indicator of genuine feelings, as individuals are often unaware of these fleeting displays.

• Deception and Truth:
   - Micro expressions are particularly relevant in the context of deception detection. Since they are not easy to control, individuals may inadvertently reveal their true feelings even when attempting to conceal them. It makes micro expressions a valuable tool for deciphering authenticity in interpersonal interactions.

• Training and Recognition:
   - Recognizing micro expressions requires training and heightened observational skills. Individuals can enhance their ability to detect these subtle cues through practice and exposure to various emotional scenarios. Training programs, often based on Ekman's work, aim to improve emotional intelligence and deception detection skills.

• Cultural Considerations:
   - While some aspects of micro expressions are universal, cultural influences may impact the interpretation of these fleeting expressions. Context and cultural norms play a role in understanding the meaning behind micro expressions, emphasizing the

importance of considering cultural diversity in their interpretation.

- Applications in Professions:
   - Professions such as law enforcement, psychology, and negotiation leverage the insights gained from micro expression analysis. Detecting subtle emotional cues aids in assessing witness credibility, understanding clients' emotional states, and improving communication in high-stakes situations.

- Real-Life Impact:
   - In everyday life, recognizing micro expressions enhances interpersonal communication. Whether in personal relationships or professional settings, the ability to decipher these fleeting expressions fosters empathy, promotes better understanding, and helps navigate social interactions more effectively.

Recognizing micro expressions is a cornerstone of emotional intelligence, contributing significantly to enhanced interpersonal understanding. Stated below are how this skill enriches emotional intelligence:

- Accurate Emotion Recognition:
   - Micro expressions provide insight into authentic emotions, allowing individuals to go beyond surface-level expressions. This accuracy in emotion

recognition is fundamental to emotional intelligence, enabling a more profound understanding of others' feelings and reactions.

• Empathy Development:
   - The ability to detect micro expressions fosters the development of empathy. By perceiving subtle emotional cues, individuals can better connect with others emotionally, demonstrating an understanding of the nuanced feelings not openly communicated.

• Responsive Communication:
   - Recognizing micro expressions empowers individuals to adjust their communication style based on the perceived emotional cues. This responsiveness ensures that interactions are tailored to the emotional needs of others, promoting more effective and empathetic communication.

• Conflict Resolution:
   - In conflict situations, understanding micro expressions allows for a deeper grasp of underlying emotions. This insight facilitates more constructive conflict resolution by addressing the root causes of emotional tension and finding mutually beneficial solutions.

• Building Trust:

- Trust and emotional intelligence are closely tied. Recognizing micro expressions enables individuals to build trust by demonstrating attentiveness and understanding of others' emotional states. It, in turn, fosters strong and more authentic connections in personal and professional relationships.

•Leadership Effectiveness:
   - Leaders with high emotional intelligence, including the ability to perceive micro expressions, are better equipped to navigate complex interpersonal dynamics. This skill aids in effective leadership by fostering a positive work environment, understanding team dynamics, and empathizing with individual team members.

• Adaptability in Communication:
   - Interpreting micro expressions allows for adaptability in communication styles. Recognizing when someone is uncomfortable or hesitant enables individuals to adjust their approach, ensuring that conversations are more considerate, inclusive, and conducive to effective collaboration.

• Enhanced Listening Skills:
   - The ability to identify micro expressions requires attentive listening and observation. It, in turn, hones

overall listening skills, enabling individuals to pick up on subtle cues that contribute to a more comprehensive understanding of others' perspectives and emotions.

• Cultural Sensitivity:
   - Recognizing micro expressions requires an awareness of cultural variations in facial expressions. This cultural sensitivity enhances emotional intelligence by considering diverse cultural contexts, preventing misunderstandings, and promoting respectful cross-cultural interactions.

• Improved Decision-Making:
   - Emotional intelligence, fueled by the recognition of micro expressions, contributes to more informed decision-making. Understanding the emotional landscape of a situation allows individuals to make decisions that consider the broader impact on relationships and team dynamics.

Recognizing micro expressions is a skill that not only deepens emotional intelligence but also positively influences interpersonal relationships, communication effectiveness, and overall well-being. It is a powerful tool for navigating the intricate nuances of the silent symphony of body language, contributing to more meaningful and authentic connections with others.

Gestures: Examination of the Language of Gestures

• Illustrators and Verbal Communication:
  - Role in Expression: Illustrators use gestures that complement and emphasize verbal communication. They accompany spoken words, adding emphasis, clarity, or emotional tone to the message. For example, hand movements while explaining a concept can enhance understanding and engagement.

  - Cultural Variations: The use and interpretation of illustrators can vary across cultures. Some cultures may incorporate more animated gestures to express enthusiasm, while others might emphasize subtler movements. Understanding these cultural nuances prevents miscommunication.

• Emblems and Cultural Variations:
  - Defining Emblems: Emblems are gestures with specific, often culturally bound meanings that can substitute for words. Examples include the "thumbs-up" or the "peace sign," which carry distinct meanings in various cultural contexts.

  - Cultural Sensitivity: Emblems can hold different connotations across cultures. While a gesture might be positive in one culture, it could be offensive or misunderstood in another. Cultural sensitivity is crucial to avoid unintentional misinterpretations and foster effective cross-cultural communication.

Adapting Gesture Use for Inclusivity and Effective Communication

• Awareness of Cultural Differences:
   - Research and Education: To adapt gesture use effectively, individuals must educate themselves about the cultural norms of the people they interact with. Researching and understanding cultural differences in body language help prevent misunderstandings and promote inclusive communication.

• Contextual Appropriateness:
   - Situational Awareness: Adapting gestures requires a keen awareness of the social and professional context. Certain gestures might be appropriate in informal settings but could be perceived differently in formal or cross-cultural environments. Contextual appropriateness ensures that gestures align with the situation at hand.

• Non-Verbal Flexibility:
   - Dynamic Adaptation: Being flexible in non-verbal communication involves adapting gestures based on the responses and cues received. If people sense

confusion or discomfort, they adjust their gestures to ensure a more inclusive and comfortable interaction.

• Avoiding Stereotypes:
   - Individual Differences: Recognizing that individuals within a culture may have diverse communication styles is crucial. Avoiding broad stereotypes and acknowledging individual differences ensures a more personalized and respectful approach to gesture use.

• Feedback and Open Communication:
   - Encouraging Dialogue: Creating an environment where individuals feel comfortable giving feedback about gestures fosters open communication. This two-way dialogue refines and adjusts non-verbal cues, ensuring a collaborative and inclusive exchange of ideas.

• Cross-Cultural Training:
   - Investing in Education: Organizations and individuals can benefit from cross-cultural training addressing non-verbal communication, including gestures. This proactive approach promotes understanding, reduces cultural barriers, and enhances inclusivity in diverse environments.

- Observation and Adaptation:
    - Learning from Observation: Paying attention to the non-verbal cues of others in a given cultural context is a valuable learning experience. Observing how gestures are applied and adapting accordingly demonstrates cultural respect and facilitates smoother communication.

Understanding the language of gestures involves recognizing the diverse roles of illustrators and emblems while acknowledging the cultural variations that influence their meaning. Adapting gesture use based on cultural context is necessary to foster inclusivity and ensure effective communication in our interconnected and multicultural world.

Posture's Silent Language

Decoding the silent messages within body posture requires a nuanced understanding of how different elements of posture convey information about power dynamics, confidence, and openness. Here's an exploration of these areas:

- Power Dynamics:
    - Dominance vs. Submissiveness: Body posture can communicate power dynamics through space

distribution. Individuals adopting expansive postures, such as open gestures and relaxed limbs, often convey dominance. Conversely, those who make themselves smaller by hunching or crossing arms may appear more submissive.

- Occupying Space: The way we occupy physical space, whether standing tall or taking a central position in a room, can signal confidence and assertiveness, contributing to perceived power.

• Confidence:

- Upright Posture: A straight and upright posture generally indicates confidence. Standing or sitting tall with shoulders back and head held high portrays self-assurance and a positive self-image.

- Gestures and Facial Expressions: Confident individuals often use purposeful and controlled gestures. Maintaining eye contact, smiling, and having a relaxed facial expression contribute to an overall impression of confidence.

• Openness:

- Open Body Language: Openness is the body language that signals receptiveness and approachability. Uncrossed arms, facing toward others, and having an open stance without physical barriers suggest a willingness to engage and connect.

- Mirroring and Synchronization: Mirroring the body language of others and synchronizing movements can create a sense of openness and rapport. It establishes a non-verbal connection that fosters positive communication.

• Insecurity and Nervousness:
   - Avoidance and Self-Touching: Insecure individuals may exhibit closed postures, avoiding eye contact, and frequently touching their face or neck. These behaviours can signal discomfort and nervousness.
   - Fidgeting: Excessive fidgeting or shifting weight from foot to foot may indicate restlessness and a lack of confidence. It may be observed as an attempt to manage anxiety or uncertainty.

• Adapting Posture for Different Contexts:
   - Professional Environments: Maintaining an upright posture and projecting confidence is often crucial. Taking up space and using expansive gestures can convey authority. However, not appearing overly dominant is necessary for fostering positive relationships.
   - Social Settings: Open and relaxed postures contribute to approachability. Mirroring the body language of others helps build rapport. Balancing confidence with humility is necessary to create a positive and inclusive atmosphere.

- Gender and Cultural Considerations:
    - Cultural Variations: Different cultures may interpret body language differently. For instance, gestures that indicate confidence in one culture may convey arrogance in another. Being aware of and respecting cultural variations is essential for effective cross-cultural communication.
    - Gender Stereotypes: Societal expectations around gender can influence body posture. Individuals may conform to or challenge these expectations, and understanding these dynamics contributes to more inclusive and equitable interactions.

Decoding body posture involves considering the holistic picture, incorporating gestures, facial expressions, and body language. It's necessary to be aware of individual differences and cultural nuances while interpreting these silent messages, ultimately fostering better communication and understanding in various social and professional contexts.

Aligning your posture for impactful communication involves intentional adjustments that convey confidence, openness, and engagement. Understanding how posture influences others' perceptions is crucial for building positive and effective interactions. Here are guides:

- Upright and Open Stance:
  - Your Posture: Stand or sit with an upright spine, conveying attentiveness and confidence. Keep your shoulders relaxed and avoid slouching. An open stance, with arms uncrossed, signals receptivity and approachability.
  - Impact on Perception: This posture exudes confidence, making you appear more assertive and self-assured. The open stance fosters a welcoming atmosphere, inviting others to engage positively and collaboratively.

- Maintain Eye Contact:
  - Your Posture: Establish and maintain eye contact with others. Avoiding excessive staring or looking down, maintain a friendly and approachable gaze.
  - Impact on Perception: Eye contact builds trust and conveys sincerity. It signals that you are actively present in the conversation, reinforcing your credibility and interest in the interaction.

- Gesture with Purpose:
  - Your Posture: Use purposeful gestures to emphasize points and convey enthusiasm. Avoid overly fidgety or distracting movements.
  - Impact on Perception: Purposeful gestures enhance verbal communication, making your message more engaging and memorable. They can

also convey passion and confidence, influencing how others perceive your level of involvement and commitment.

• Mirroring and Synchronization:
   - Your Posture: Subtly mirror the body language of others to create a sense of connection. Align your posture with the tone and pace of the conversation.
   - Impact on Perception: Mirroring fosters rapport and a feeling of connection. It indicates empathy and adaptability, making others more receptive to your communication.

• Adapt Posture to Context:
   - Your Posture: Be mindful of the context in which you communicate. In professional settings, maintain a balance between confidence and humility. In social situations, focus on creating an open and friendly atmosphere.
   - Impact on Perception: Adapting your posture to the context ensures you are confident and approachable. It demonstrates social intelligence and an understanding of situational dynamics.

• Project Vocal Confidence:
   - Your Posture: Stand or sit up straight to support vocal projection. Speak clearly and at a moderate pace.

- Impact on Perception: A confident posture enhances the quality of your voice and how others perceive your communication skills. It contributes to an authoritative and compelling presence.

• Minimize Defensive Postures:
  - Your Posture: Avoid defensive postures, such as crossing arms or creating physical barriers. Keep your body language open and inviting.
  - Impact on Perception: Defensive postures can create a sense of distance and defensiveness. Open posture invites trust and promotes a more collaborative and positive exchange of ideas.

• Cultural Sensitivity:
  - Your Posture: Be aware of cultural variations in body language and adjust your posture accordingly.
  - Impact on Perception: Adapting your posture to align with cultural norms demonstrates respect and inclusivity, fostering a more positive and understanding perception of your communication style.

Aligning your posture for impactful communication involves a conscious effort to convey confidence, openness, and engagement. Understanding how posture influences others' perceptions allows you to build stronger connections, facilitate effective communication, and leave a positive impression in various personal and professional interactions.

Cultural Sensitivity:

- Emphasizing Cultural Awareness in Interpreting Body Language:
• Cultural Variability in Body Language:
   - Different cultures may ascribe varied meanings to the same body language cues. For example, direct eye contact may be a sign of confidence in one culture but perceived as confrontational or disrespectful in another. Recognizing these variations is essential for accurate interpretation.

• Cultural Display Rules:
   - Cultural display rules dictate the appropriateness and intensity of expressing emotions through body language. Some cultures encourage more expressive gestures, while others prioritize restraint. Understanding these rules helps prevent misinterpretations and ensures respectful engagement.

• Diverse Interpretations of Gestures:
   - Gestures, whether illustrators or emblems, can carry distinct meanings across cultures. A seemingly innocent gesture in one culture may be offensive or inappropriate in another. Cultural awareness is

crucial to avoid misunderstandings and navigate diverse social landscapes successfully.

- Guidelines to Seamlessly Steer through Cultural Differences in Body Language:

• Educate Yourself:
   - Before engaging with individuals from different cultures, invest time learning about their cultural norms and body language expectations. Cultural sensitivity training or resources specific to the region can provide valuable insights.

• Observe and Learn:
   - Pay attention to the body language of locals when in a new cultural setting. Observe how people express themselves non-verbally, including gestures, facial expressions, and posture. This observational learning aids in adapting to cultural nuances.

• Ask for Guidance:
   - When in doubt, seek guidance from local colleagues, friends, or guides. They can offer valuable insights into cultural norms and expectations, helping you navigate interactions more effectively.

- Mind Your Proxemics:
  - Proxemics, the use of personal space, varies widely across cultures. Some cultures value proximity during conversations, while others prefer more distance. Being mindful of these preferences ensures a comfortable and respectful interaction.

- Respect Non-Verbal Cues:
  - Respect cues related to non-verbal communication, such as facial expressions and gestures. If someone looks uncomfortable or hesitant, adjust your approach to create a more inclusive and respectful environment.

- Adapt Your Non-Verbal Behaviour:
  - Be open to adapting your non-verbal behaviour to align with cultural expectations. It includes modifying gestures, adjusting your level of eye contact, and being mindful of your posture to convey respect and cultural sensitivity.

- Consider Gender Dynamics:
  - Some cultures may have specific expectations regarding the non-verbal behaviour of men and women. Be aware of these gender dynamics to avoid unintentional breaches of cultural norms.

- Learn About Taboos:

- Familiarize yourself with cultural taboos related to body language. Certain gestures or postures may carry negative connotations or be considered disrespectful. Knowing and avoiding these taboos is crucial for maintaining positive interactions.

• Be Patient and Reflective:
  - In unfamiliar cultural settings, patience is necessary. Take the time to reflect on your non-verbal cues and adapt as needed. Being open to learning and adjusting fosters cross-cultural understanding.

By emphasizing cultural awareness and implementing practical tips, individuals can navigate the complexities of cultural differences in body language. It promotes respectful and inclusive communication and adds to building positive relationships across diverse cultural contexts.

The Interplay of Signals

Exploring the Harmony of Gestures, Expressions, and Posture:
• Coordinated Non-Verbal Communication:
  - Ineffective communication, gestures, expressions, and posture convey complex messages. For example, a person expressing excitement may use animated gestures, a smiling facial expression, and

an upright posture, collectively creating a coherent and enthusiastic message.

• Emotional Consistency:
  - When non-verbal cues align, they reinforce the emotional content of a message. A person expressing sadness may exhibit a slouched posture, lowered gaze, and subtle gestures like covering the face, providing a consistent and powerful expression of their emotional state.

• Complementary Roles:
  - Gestures often complement spoken words, enhancing the clarity and impact of the message. Likewise, expressions and posture contribute additional layers of meaning, enriching the communication experience. The synergy of these elements allows for a more nuanced and comprehensive expression of thoughts and emotions.

• Contextual Adaptation:
  - The interplay of gestures, expressions, and posture adapts to different contexts. In a professional setting, confident gestures, a composed facial expression, and an upright posture may convey authority. In contrast, a casual social setting may involve more relaxed gestures, a warm expression, and an open posture, fostering a friendly atmosphere.

Analyzing Real-Life Scenarios:

• Job Interview:
  - Gestures: During a job interview, appropriate gestures such as nodding in agreement or using open-handed gestures can convey engagement and confidence.
  - Expressions: Facial expressions reflecting genuine interest and enthusiasm add positively to the interviewer's perception.
  - Posture: Sitting upright with a relaxed yet attentive posture communicates professionalism and preparedness.

• Cross-Cultural Business Meeting:
  - Gestures: Understanding culturally appropriate gestures is crucial. In some cultures, pointing may be considered impolite, while in others, it may be a common and accepted practice.
  - Expressions: Facial expressions indicating respect, such as maintaining a neutral or slightly positive expression, contribute to positive cross-cultural communication.
  - Posture: Adapting posture to align with cultural norms, such as sitting or standing at an appropriate distance, enhances understanding and fosters inclusivity.

- Conflict Resolution:
    - Gestures: Open and non-threatening gestures can ease tension during conflict resolution. Avoiding aggressive gestures contributes to a more collaborative atmosphere.
    - Expressions: Maintaining a calm and composed facial expression helps de-escalate conflicts and encourages constructive dialogue.
    - Posture: A neutral and approachable posture, avoiding defensive positions, supports a more open and understanding environment for conflict resolution.

- Social Gathering:
    - Gestures: Animated and expressive gestures may be more common in a casual social setting, contributing to a lively and engaging atmosphere.
    - Expressions: Facial expressions reflecting joy, interest, or humour contribute positively to the social dynamics of the gathering.
    - Posture: A relaxed and open posture fosters a sense of camaraderie and approachability, encouraging social interactions.

- Leadership Address:
    - Gestures: Purposeful and authoritative gestures enhance the impact of a leader's address, conveying confidence and emphasizing key points.

- Expressions: Expressing sincerity and empathy through facial expressions fosters a connection between the leader and the audience.
- Posture: A commanding yet inclusive posture, for example, standing tall and maintaining eye contact, reinforces the leader's authority while remaining approachable.

In these scenarios, the interconnectedness of gestures, expressions, and posture becomes evident, influencing perceptions and shaping the overall communication experience. Understanding this harmony is crucial for effective communication in diverse social contexts, allowing individuals to convey complex messages with authenticity and impact.

Chapter Four

Engaging Small Talk as Bridges to Understanding - Unveiling the Secrets of Transformative, Meaningful Exchanges

As we commence to unravel the profound dynamics of human connection, we delve into the intricate art of small talk – a simple activity that serves as a powerful bridge to understanding. Within the seemingly casual exchanges of everyday chatter lies the potential for transformative and meaningful connections.

The Power of Casual Conversation
Small talk, often dismissed as inconsequential banter, plays a crucial role in breaking down social barriers. It acts as the initial thread that weaves the fabric of connection, providing a platform for individuals to find common ground. Through discussions about the weather, shared experiences, or even a mutual interest in the latest news, participants unknowingly lay the foundation for more profound interactions.

Navigating Light Topics for Deeper Bonds
In the realm of small talk, the selection of topics is an art. Navigating through light and relatable subjects is an art that requires finesse and an understanding of

the intricacies of human interaction. Here, readers will explore the subtle techniques that can transform seemingly casual conversations into meaningful exchanges by steering them toward areas of shared interest.

- Identifying Shared Interests

Accepting that individuals are different, we encourage readers to observe and identify shared interests during small talk. Whether it's a passion for a particular hobby, an appreciation for a cultural aspect, or a mutual fascination with a trending topic, recognizing these shared elements becomes the compass for guiding the conversation.

- Crafting Open-Ended Questions

To skillfully steer conversations, we emphasize the use of open-ended questions. Instead of inquiring with a simple "yes" or "no" response in mind, readers learn to pose questions that invite detailed and thoughtful answers. This approach not only keeps the conversation flowing but also provides opportunities for participants to share more about their perspectives and experiences.

- Creating a Comfortable Atmosphere

A crucial aspect of navigating conversations toward shared interests is establishing a comfortable atmosphere. It involves adopting a friendly tone, maintaining positive body language, and conveying a genuine interest in the other person's preferences.

- Pivoting with Grace
Small talk often involves navigating various topics before finding common ground. By seamlessly weaving related subjects into the dialogue, individuals can guide the flow of the conversation toward more meaningful territory.

- Flexibility in Conversation Dynamics
Recognizing that conversations are dynamic, we advise readers to be flexible in steering discussions. Sometimes, the natural flow may take unexpected turns, and readers are encouraged to adapt without losing sight of shared interests. This flexibility allows for organic and authentic exchanges, fostering an understanding between participants.

- Building Rapport Through Shared Experiences
As readers navigate conversations toward shared interests, we underscore the importance of shared experiences. Whether it's reminiscing about an event, discussing a hobby, or exploring mutual goals, building rapport through shared experiences solidifies the connection and sets the stage for more profound exchanges.

Active Listening: A Gateway to Deeper Understanding

Central to the secrets of transformative exchanges is the skill of active listening. We underscore the importance of not merely hearing but truly understanding the nuances of conversation. Maintaining eye contact, nodding in agreement, and posing open-ended questions are recommended to enhance the reader's ability to engage in meaningful dialogue.

Authenticity and Vulnerability

To unlock the transformative potential of exchanges, we encourage readers to embrace authenticity and vulnerability in their communication. Sharing personal experiences fosters a deeper connection and opens the door to a more profound exchange of ideas and perspectives. The realization that each person brings a unique story to the table contributes to the richness of the interaction.

The Role of Empathy

A cornerstone of meaningful exchanges is empathy. By putting oneself in the shoes of the conversation partner, individuals can navigate conversations with compassion and sensitivity, further enhancing the transformative nature of the exchange.

This chapter serves as a guide to the subtle yet potent world of small talk. It demonstrates how these seemingly insignificant conversations act as bridges, connecting individuals and laying the groundwork for transformative and meaningful exchanges. Through active listening, authenticity, vulnerability, and empathy, readers unlock the secrets of profound human connection in the seemingly mundane moments of everyday conversation.

Chapter Five

Building a Solid Framework for Rapport - Foundations of Good Communication Laid Bare

In the intricate tapestry of meaningful connections, this chapter delves into the essential task of constructing a robust framework for rapport. As we lay bare the foundations of good communication, readers will explore the fundamental elements that build strong and enduring connections.

Understanding the Dynamics of Rapport

Before delving into the building process, this chapter sheds light on the dynamics of rapport. Understanding the reciprocity of communication is akin to recognizing that meaningful interaction is a mutual exchange where both participants contribute to the flow of conversation. In this context, the street of communication is a shared pathway where ideas, thoughts, and emotions travel in both directions. Let's delve deeper into the dynamics of this two-way street:

- Mutual Contribution
Reciprocity underscores that communication involves active participation from all parties involved. It's not

just about one person expressing themselves while the other passively listens; it's a collaborative effort where both individuals contribute to the dialogue. Acknowledging this reciprocity encourages a balanced and engaging exchange.

- Shared Responsibility for Understanding

On the two-way street of communication, both parties share the responsibility of ensuring understanding. It goes beyond merely speaking and listening – it involves actively seeking comprehension. Participants are encouraged to clarify points, ask questions, and confirm their understanding, fostering an environment where both perspectives are valued and acknowledged.

- Responsive Interaction

Reciprocity manifests in the responsiveness of communication. It's about being attuned to the verbal and non-verbal cues provided by the conversation partner. A back-and-forth exchange involves thoughtful responses, creating a dynamic and fluid conversation where each person's input is acknowledged and responded to, fostering a sense of connection.

- Co-Creation of Meaning

Communication is not a one-sided delivery of information; it is a collaborative process of co-creating meaning. It involves both parties actively shaping and interpreting the content of the conversation. By recognizing the shared responsibility for constructing meaning, individuals contribute to a more nuanced and enriched exchange.

- Building Connection through Reciprocal Disclosure
Reciprocity extends to the sharing of personal information. It's not just about one person revealing their thoughts and experiences; it's a reciprocal process where both individuals gradually disclose aspects of themselves. This mutual sharing fosters a deeper understanding and connection, creating a sense of intimacy and trust on the shared street of communication.

- Balancing Power Dynamics
Acknowledging the two-way street of communication helps balance power dynamics in conversations. It promotes an environment where everyone's voice is valued, ensuring no party dominates the exchange. This balance contributes to more inclusive and respectful communication, where each participant feels heard and acknowledged.
Understanding the give-and-take nature of rapport is pivotal to establishing a foundation that withstands the test of time.

Authenticity as the Cornerstone

At the heart of building rapport lies authenticity. The transformative power of being true to oneself and cultivating an environment where others feel comfortable doing the same is a profound journey toward authenticity and genuine connection. In this exploration, you will discover how embracing one's true self and fostering such authenticity in others can lead to transformative experiences and meaningful relationships.

- Embracing Personal Authenticity

We explore the notion that authenticity begins with self-discovery and self-acceptance. Authenticity encourages individuals to embrace their values, beliefs, and individuality without succumbing to societal expectations or external pressures. By acknowledging and celebrating their authentic selves, individuals pave the way for a more genuine and fulfilling life.

- Creating a Safe Space for Vulnerability

We emphasize the importance of creating a safe and non-judgmental space for vulnerability. Real connections often emerge when individuals feel secure enough to share their thoughts, emotions, and experiences. Fostering such an environment encourages openness and strengthens the bonds between people.

- Encouraging Honest Communication

The transformative power lies in fostering honest and transparent communication. Navigating conversations with sincerity to foster an atmosphere of trust and understanding involves mindful communication and genuine engagement. Here are practical guidance to help readers navigate conversations authentically:

• Active Listening:
  - Practice Presence: Be fully present in the conversation, eliminating distractions and actively focusing on the speaker.
  - Non-Verbal Cues: Demonstrate attentiveness through non-verbal cues like maintaining eye contact, nodding, and using affirmative gestures.

• Open and Honest Expression:
  - Share Genuine Thoughts: Express your thoughts and feelings sincerely, avoiding pretence or exaggeration.
  - Use "I" Statements: Frame statements using "I" to convey personal experiences, making your communication more authentic and less accusatory.

• Ask Thoughtful Questions:

- Open-Ended Queries: Pose open-ended questions that elicit the other person to share more about their perspectives and experiences.
  - Reflective Questions: Ask questions that reflect your genuine interest in understanding the other person's point of view.

• Validate Emotions:
  - Empathetic Responses: Acknowledge and validate the emotions expressed by others, showing empathy and understanding.
  - Avoid Judgement: Refrain from passing judgment on the emotions or experiences shared by maintaining an open and non-critical attitude.

• Be conscious of and Body Language and Tone:
  - Positive Tone: Use a positive and respectful tone that aligns with the sincerity of your message.
  - Open Body Language: Ensure your body language reflects openness and honesty, avoiding defensive postures.

• Clarify and Confirm:
  - Seek Clarification: Ask for clarification rather than making assumptions if something seems unclear.

- Confirm Understanding: Periodically summarize key points to confirm understanding and demonstrate active engagement.

• Share Personal Experiences:
- Vulnerability: When appropriate, share relevant personal experiences to create a deeper connection and demonstrate authenticity.
- Relatability: Connect your experiences to the conversation, emphasizing common ground and shared understanding.

• Respectful Feedback:
- Constructive Feedback: If offering feedback, do so constructively and with respect, focusing on specific behaviours or actions rather than making generalized judgments.
- Encourage Feedback: provide an enabling environment where others are at ease giving their feedback.

• Cultivate Trust Over Time:
- Consistency: Be consistent in your communication and actions over time to build a sense of reliability.
- Follow Through: If you commit to something, follow through on your promises, reinforcing trust in your reliability.

• Admit Mistakes:

- Ownership: If you make a mistake, admit it openly, take responsibility and demonstrate a commitment to learning and improving.
  - Apologize Sincerely: Offer sincere apologies when needed, expressing genuine remorse.

By incorporating these practical guidelines into conversations, readers can confidently navigate discussions, contributing to an atmosphere of trust and understanding. This approach establishes a foundation for more meaningful and authentic connections in both personal and professional relationships.

Building Trust Through Authenticity
Trust is a cornerstone of meaningful relationships. By consistently being true to oneself and encouraging others to do the same, individuals create a foundation of reliability and integrity. Trust becomes the currency of genuine connections, unlocking the door to more profound and transformative interactions.

Nurturing a Culture of Acceptance
Fostering an environment where authenticity is encouraged contributes to a culture of acceptance. It involves embracing diversity of thought, experiences, and perspectives.

The transformative impact of accepting others for who they are is a powerful concept that goes beyond mere tolerance—it embraces diversity, cultivates empathy, and fosters a sense of belonging and inclusion. Below are the profound effects of embracing authenticity in others:

- Cultivating Empathy:
  - Understanding Diverse Perspectives: Acceptance involves recognizing and understanding the unique perspectives, experiences, and backgrounds of others.
  - Empathetic Connection: By embracing authenticity, individuals cultivate empathy, forging deeper connections based on a genuine understanding of each other's journeys.

- Fostering Inclusivity:
  - Creating an Inclusive Environment: Acceptance creates an inclusive atmosphere where individuals feel valued and respected for their authentic selves.
  - Encouraging Participation: People are more likely to actively engage in conversations and activities if they feel accepted, contributing to a diverse and vibrant community.

- Building Trust and Rapport:
  - Foundation of Trust: Accepting others builds a foundation of trust. When individuals feel accepted,

they are more likely to trust and connect with those around them.
   - Deepening Rapport: Authentic connections flourish in an environment of acceptance, deepening rapport and fostering a sense of camaraderie.

• Enhancing Psychological Safety:
   - Encouraging Openness: Acceptance creates a psychologically safe space where individuals feel comfortable expressing their thoughts and feelings without fear of judgment.
   - Reducing Fear of Rejection: When people know they are accepted, they are more likely to share their authentic selves, reducing the fear of rejection.

• Promoting Individual Growth:
   - Encouraging Self-Expression: Acceptance encourages individuals to express themselves authentically, fostering personal growth and self-discovery.
   - Creating a Nurturing Environment: An atmosphere of acceptance nurtures individual strengths, talents, and potential, promoting continuous development.

• Strengthens Interpersonal Relationships:
   - Deeper Connections: Accepting others for who they are leads to deeper and more meaningful connections in friendships, family relationships, and professional collaborations.

- Mutual Respect: Acceptance fosters mutual respect, creating a positive and supportive foundation for interpersonal relationships.

- Breaking Down Stereotypes and Biases:
  - Challenging Assumptions: Acceptance challenges preconceived notions and biases, encouraging individuals to see beyond stereotypes and appreciate the richness of diversity.
  - Promoting Understanding: By accepting others' authentic selves, individuals gain a more nuanced understanding of different perspectives, fostering cultural competence.

- Promoting a Sense of Belonging:
  - Inclusive Communities: Acceptance contributes to inclusive communities where everyone feels a sense of belonging.
  - Valued Contributions: When individuals feel accepted, they are more likely to contribute their unique skills and perspectives, enriching the collective experience.

- Inspiring Positive Change:
  - Catalyst for Transformation: Acceptance is a catalyst for positive social change by challenging norms and promoting a culture of respect and understanding.

- Creating a Ripple Effect: Individual acceptance can inspire others to embrace diversity, creating a ripple effect that transcends individual interactions.

In essence, the transformative impact of accepting others for who they are extends far beyond the immediate relationships—it has the potential to shape communities, organizations, and societies by fostering an environment where authenticity is encouraged, diversity is the norm, and individuals feel a profound sense of belonging and inclusion.

Empathy and Understanding
The transformative journey of authenticity involves expressing oneself genuinely and understanding and empathizing with the authenticity of others. Cultivating empathy creates a reciprocal environment where individuals feel seen, heard, and valued. This mutual understanding deepens connections and fosters a sense of shared humanity.

Unlocking Personal Growth
Embracing authenticity leads to personal growth. By being true to yourself and fostering authenticity in your relationships, you create opportunities for self-discovery, resilience, and continuous development. Authenticity becomes a catalyst for transformative experiences that shape both individual lives and the connections between people.

The transformative power of being true to oneself and cultivating authenticity in relationships is a journey of self-discovery, vulnerability, honest communication, trust-building, acceptance, empathy, and personal growth. By understanding and embracing authenticity, readers embark on a path that enriches their lives and fosters meaningful connections with others.

Effective Listening Techniques

Building understanding necessitates a keen focus on effective listening. From active listening to empathetic understanding, the art of hearing and comprehending the nuance of communication is unveiled. Through active listening, individuals can forge deeper connections by acknowledging and validating the thoughts and feelings of others.

Verbal and Non-Verbal Communication

The interplay between verbal and non-verbal communication is a dynamic and intricate dance that significantly influences the overall message conveyed in interpersonal interactions. Understanding how these two forms of communication complement and sometimes contradict each other is crucial for effective and nuanced communication. Here's a deeper exploration of this interplay:

- Conveying Emotions:
  - Verbal Expression: Words can express emotions, but might not always capture the full depth of feelings.
  - Non-Verbal Cues: Facial expressions, body language, and gestures provide additional layers to emotional expression, offering insights into sincerity, enthusiasm, or distress.

- Clarifying Ambiguous Messages:
  - Verbal Clarity: Verbal communication conveys explicit information, but messages can sometimes be ambiguous.
  - Non-Verbal Cues: Non-verbal signals, such as tone of voice or gestures, can clarify the intended meaning or emphasize specific points, reducing ambiguity.

- Emphasizing Key Points:
  - Verbal Emphasis: Through the choice of words and tone, verbal communication emphasizes points.
  - Non-Verbal Reinforcement: Non-verbal cues, like nodding or hand gestures, can reinforce or underscore the significance of verbal messages, adding weight to points.

- Building Trust and Credibility:

- Verbal Consistency: Verbal messages contribute to the perceived credibility of a speaker.
  - Non-Verbal Trust Indicators: Non-verbal cues, like maintaining eye contact, posture, and facial expressions, play a crucial role in building trust and credibility, sometimes even more than spoken words.

• Expressing Agreement or Disagreement:
  - Verbal Affirmation: Verbal agreement or disagreement is explicit through spoken words.
  - Non-Verbal Confirmation: Non-verbal cues, such as head nodding or shaking, can silently affirm or challenge verbal statements, adding nuance to the conversation.

• Navigating Cultural Differences:
  - Verbal Language Variances: Different cultures may have diverse verbal expressions and idioms.
  - Non-Verbal Universals: Some non-verbal cues, like facial expressions or body language, can be more universally understood, helping bridge language gaps and facilitating cross-cultural communication.

• Detecting Deception:
  - Verbal Inconsistencies: Deceptive messages might contain verbal inconsistencies.
  - Non-Verbal Clues: Non-verbal cues like changes in facial expressions, body movements, or avoiding

eye contact, can indicate potential deception, providing additional insights.

• Enhancing Engagement:
  - Verbal Engagement: Engaging language is vital to captivate an audience.
  - Non-Verbal Engagement: Non-verbal cues, like maintaining a dynamic posture or using expressive facial expressions, complement verbal engagement, making communication more captivating.

• Establishing Rapport:
  - Verbal Warmth: Verbal expressions of warmth and friendliness contribute to rapport.
  - Non-Verbal Affection: Non-verbal cues, such as smiling, a friendly tone, or appropriate touch, further establish a positive and welcoming atmosphere, deepening connections.

• Resolving Conflict:
  - Verbal Resolution: Conflict resolution involves verbal negotiation and compromise.
  - Non-Verbal Reassurance: Non-verbal cues, such as open body language or a reassuring touch, can convey sincerity and contribute to the emotional resolution of conflicts.

The interplay between verbal and non-verbal communication is an interconnected dance that adds layers of meaning to human interaction. By recognizing and understanding this interplay, individuals can enhance their communication skills, fostering clearer understanding, building stronger connections, and navigating the complexities of human relationships more effectively.

Building Consistency in Communication
Consistency is necessary for any successful rapport-building endeavour. It is required to maintain a consistent communication style and reliability in interactions. Predictable and reliable communication fosters a sense of security, contributing to the development of a solid framework for rapport.

- Navigating Challenges in Communication
Navigating communication challenges requires a combination of self-awareness, active listening, and adaptive strategies. Here are some strategies to overcome communication challenges:

• Active Listening:
   - Focused Attention: Actively concentrate on what the other person is saying without interrupting.
   - Paraphrasing: Repeat or paraphrase what you've heard to confirm understanding and show that you are actively engaged.

• Empathy and Understanding:

- Put Yourself in Their Shoes: Try to understand the situation from the other person's perspective.
  - Express Empathy: Acknowledge their feelings and emotions to demonstrate understanding and validate their experiences.

- Open Communication:
  - Encourage Openness: Create an environment where individuals feel comfortable expressing their thoughts and concerns.
  - Ask for Feedback: Invite constructive feedback to understand the other person's perspective.

- Clarity in Expression:
  - Use Clear and Concise Language: Avoid ambiguity by expressing yourself clearly and concisely.
  - Avoid Assumptions: Confirm that your message is understood by encouraging questions and seeking clarification.

- Non-verbal awareness:
  - Pay Attention to Body Language: Be mindful of non-verbal cues, such as facial expressions and posture, to gauge the other person's reactions.
  - Adapt Your Non-Verbal Communication: Adjust your non-verbal cues to convey openness and receptivity.

- Stay Calm and Composed:
  - Manage Emotional Responses: Keep emotions in check to prevent conflicts from escalating.
  - Take a Pause if Necessary: Taking a momentary break can help both parties cool down if the conversation becomes intense.

- Clarification and Summarization:
  - Seek Clarification: If there's confusion, ask for clarification on specific points.
  - Summarize Key Points: Summarize the main points of the conversation to ensure alignment on essential details.

- Use Positive Language:
  - Frame Messages Positively: Use positive language to convey your thoughts and intentions.
  - Avoid Blame: Focus on solutions rather than placing blame to create a more collaborative atmosphere.

- Adapt Communication Style:
  - Recognize Different Communication Styles: Understand that people have varied communication styles.

- Adapt to Their Style: Adjust your approach to align with the other person's preferred style for better understanding.

• Conflict Resolution Techniques:
  - Problem-Solving: Work together on finding solutions to issues.
  - Seek Compromise: Be willing to find a middle ground and compromise to meet the needs of all parties involved.

• Feedback Loops:
  - Encourage Feedback: Establish a culture of continuous feedback to improve communication over time.
  - Learn from Miscommunications: Use past challenges as learning opportunities to enhance future interactions.

• Cultural Sensitivity:
  - Knowing differences in cultures: Get informed about cultural differences that may impact communication.
  - Adapt Communication to Cultural Context: Adjust your communication style to respect and accommodate diverse cultural perspectives.

• Professional Mediation:

- Involve a Neutral Third Party: Where challenges persist, consider involving a professional mediator to facilitate communication and resolution.

• Reflective Practice:
  - Self-Reflection: Regularly reflect on your communication style and identify areas for improvement.
  - Adapt Based on Feedback: Be open to adjusting your communication strategies based on feedback received.

By integrating these strategies into your communication approach, you can navigate challenges effectively, foster better understanding, and contribute to a more positive and collaborative communication environment.

Fostering Mutual Respect
Rapport flourishes in an environment of mutual respect. It is important to treat others with dignity and value diverse perspectives. Fostering a culture of respect lays the groundwork for robust connections, encouraging open and constructive communication.

This chapter has served as a comprehensive guide to building a solid framework for rapport. By understanding the dynamics of rapport, embracing authenticity, honing effective listening techniques, mastering the interplay of verbal and non-verbal communication, building consistency, navigating challenges, and fostering mutual respect, readers are equipped to construct enduring connections founded on the principles of good communication.

Chapter Six

Navigating the Profound Waters of Connection - Unlocking the Potential for Richer, More Fulfilling Relationships

This chapter navigates the complexities of interpersonal bonds, unlocking the potential for more fulfilling relationships.

Understanding the Layers of Connection
Understanding the layers of connection involves recognizing the varying degrees of intimacy and emotional depth that characterize relationships. From casual acquaintanceships to deeper, more intimate connections, each layer contributes to the diverse landscape of human interactions. Let's delve deeper into these layers:

• Casual Acquaintanceships:
   - Surface Interactions: At this level, connections are composed of surface-level interactions and minimal personal disclosure.
   - Limited Shared Experiences: Individuals in casual acquaintanceships engage in polite conversations and share minimal aspects of their lives.

• Friendly Connections:

- Common Interests: As connections improve, individuals may discover shared interests, forming a basis for more amiable interactions.
  - Occasional Socializing: Friendship involves occasional socializing, mostly in group settings or during specific events.

- Colleague or Professional Relationships:
  - Shared Goals: In professional contexts, relationships often revolve around shared goals and collaborative efforts.
  - Task-Oriented Interaction: Interactions are about work-related tasks, with limited personal sharing.

- Close Friendships:
  - Increased Vulnerability: Close friendships involve higher vulnerability and personal disclosure.
  - Emotional Support: Individuals in close friendships provide emotional support and share a significant portion of their lives.

- Romantic Relationships:
  - Intimate Emotional Bonds: Romantic connections entail a deep emotional bond and often include shared goals and plans.
  - Physical Intimacy: These relationships may involve physical intimacy, further deepening the connection.

- Committed Partnerships:
  - Long-Term Commitment: Committed partnerships signify a long-term commitment, often including shared living arrangements and life responsibilities.
  - Shared Future: Individuals in committed partnerships plan their futures together, with joint decision-making and mutual support.

- Familial Bonds:
  - Inherent Connection: Familial bonds are inherent, often rooted in blood relationships.
  - Lifelong Support: Family connections involve a lifelong support system, with a shared history and a sense of obligation.

- Deep Intimacy and Soul Connections:
  - Spiritual or Soul Connections: This level transcends the physical and emotional, involving a deep, spiritual, or soulful connection.
  - Profound Understanding: Individuals in such connections share unparalleled understanding and resonance.

- Life Partnerships:
  - Unified Life Paths: Life partnerships involve individuals sharing every aspect of their lives, from daily routines to long-term goals.

- Unwavering Commitment: These connections are composed of unwavering commitment and a shared journey through life's challenges and triumphs.

• Soulmates and Twin Flames:
  - Rare, Profound Connections: Soulmates and twin flames represent rare and profound connections.
  - Spiritual Synchronicity: These connections are often described as spiritually synchronized and transformative, involving a deep sense of completeness.

Understanding the layers of connection allows individuals to navigate relationships with awareness and intention. Recognizing where a connection falls on this spectrum helps to set appropriate expectations, foster mutual understanding, and navigate the journey of human connections with authenticity and depth. Each layer contributes to the richness and complexity of the relational landscape, offering unique opportunities for growth and fulfillment.

The Role of Vulnerability in Deepening Bonds
- Embracing Vulnerability:
Vulnerability is the raw and authentic expression of one's thoughts, emotions, and true self, even in uncertainty or potential discomfort. In the context of

forging profound connections, embracing vulnerability has transformative power.

- Authentic Connection: Vulnerability fosters authentic connections by allowing individuals to show their true selves without being judged. When people share their vulnerabilities, it creates a space for genuine understanding and empathy.

- Deepening Intimacy: In relationships, friendships, or romantic partnerships, vulnerability is a yardstick for deepening intimacy. Sharing personal fears, insecurities, and dreams creates a profound bond beyond surface-level interactions.

- Mutual Trust: Vulnerability builds trust. When individuals are willing to expose their vulnerabilities, it signals trust in the other person. This reciprocal sharing of vulnerabilities creates a foundation of trust, essential for profound connections.

- Encourages Reciprocity: If a party reveals areas of vulnerability about himself, it encourages the other party to talk about himself also. This mutual vulnerability fosters a shared experience, creating a sense of equality and understanding in the relationship.

- Emotional Resonance: Vulnerability allows for emotional resonance, where individuals connect on a deep emotional level. It enables the confirmation of shared human experiences, creating a sense of unity and compassion.

Creating Safe Spaces:
Creating a safe space involves cultivating an environment where individuals feel accepted, valued, and secure enough to express their true selves without fear of judgment or reprisal. It is crucial for fostering meaningful connections.

- Encourages Openness: A safe space encourages open communication. When individuals feel safe, they are more likely to express their thoughts, feelings, and ideas freely, contributing to more honest and transparent interactions.

- Promotes Authenticity: Safe spaces allow individuals to be authentic and genuine without fear of criticism. This authenticity enhances the quality of connections, as people feel comfortable being themselves.

- Facilitates Emotional Expression: Emotional expression is vital in connections. Creating a safe space enables individuals to express a wide range of emotions, fostering a deeper understanding of each other's experiences.

- Reduces Fear of Rejection: In a safe space, the fear of rejection is minimized. Individuals can share vulnerabilities and unique aspects of their identity without worrying about being judged or ostracized.

- Strengthens Trust: Safe spaces contribute to the development of trust within relationships. When individuals know they are in an environment where their thoughts and feelings are respected, it strengthens the foundation of trust.

- Supports Growth and Exploration: Safe spaces provide room for personal and interpersonal growth. Individuals are more likely to explore new ideas, perspectives, and aspects of themselves when they feel secure in their environment.

- Enhances Collaboration: Creating a safe space fosters collaboration in professional settings. Team members share innovative ideas and work together effectively when the workplace is conducive to open communication.

Embracing vulnerability and creating safe spaces are interconnected elements in the journey of forging profound connections. Vulnerability unlocks the depth of relationships, while safe spaces provide the nurturing ground where these connections can flourish and endure. Together, they form the cornerstone of authentic and transformative human interactions.

Cultivating Emotional Intelligence

Understanding Emotions and Emotional Intelligence: Emotional intelligence (EI) is the ability to recognize, understand, manage, and effectively use one's emotions, as well as being attuned to the emotions of others. In the context of building deeper connections, a high level of emotional intelligence plays a pivotal role:

- Self-Awareness: Emotional intelligence begins with self-awareness, the ability to recognize and understand one's emotions. When individuals are attuned to their feelings, they can navigate their emotional landscape more effectively, contributing to more authentic interactions.

- Self-Regulation: The capacity to manage and regulate emotions is another crucial aspect of emotional intelligence. This self-regulation prevents impulsive reactions and allows individuals to respond thoughtfully in social situations, promoting smoother and more harmonious connections.

- Empathy: Empathy is a central component of emotional intelligence, which involves understanding and sharing the feelings of others. By recognizing and resonating with the emotions of those around us, individuals with high emotional intelligence can establish a deeper understanding and connection with others.

- Social Skills: Emotional intelligence enhances social skills, enabling individuals to navigate interpersonal relationships more effectively. Social skills involve effective communication, conflict resolution, building and maintaining positive connections with others.

- Motivation: Individuals with high emotional intelligence are often motivated by intrinsic factors. This internal motivation contributes to perseverance, resilience, and a positive outlook, all of which contribute to building and sustaining meaningful connections.

Empathy and Connection:
Empathy, as a component of emotional intelligence, plays a vital role in building and enriching connections.

- Understanding Others: Empathy involves the ability to understand the perspectives, emotions, and experiences of others. This understanding creates a foundation for deeper connections by demonstrating a genuine interest in the well-being of those around us.

- Validation and Support: Empathy goes beyond understanding; it includes validating and acknowledging the emotions of others. When individuals feel heard and understood, it fosters a sense of connection and emotional support, contributing to the overall quality of relationships.

- Building Trust: Empathy is a powerful tool for building trust. When individuals sense that others genuinely care about their feelings and experiences, it establishes a foundation of trust and mutual understanding, essential for the longevity of connections.

- Conflict Resolution: In times of conflict, empathy allows individuals to see multiple perspectives and find common ground. This empathetic approach to conflict resolution promotes understanding and helps maintain positive connections even during challenging times.

- Enhancing Communication: Empathy enhances the quality of communication by encouraging active listening and a more thoughtful response. When individuals feel understood and valued, it creates an environment where communication flows more smoothly, fostering deep connections.

- Cultural Sensitivity: Empathy is integral in understanding and appreciating cultural differences. It allows individuals to navigate diverse perspectives, contributing to the creation of inclusive and culturally sensitive connections.

Understanding emotions through emotional intelligence and practicing empathy are intertwined with building deeper connections. Emotional intelligence provides the foundational skills for navigating one's emotions and those of others, while empathy enriches relationships by fostering understanding, validation, trust, and effective communication. Together, they create a framework for authentic and meaningful human connections.

• **Building Bridges Across Differences**

Appreciating Diversity:
Appreciating diversity in relationships involves recognizing and valuing differences in various aspects, such as cultural background, perspectives, experiences, and individual traits. Accepting diversity improves connections.

- Cultural Enrichment: Diversity introduces different cultural perspectives, traditions, and practices into relationships, providing an opportunity for cultural enrichment and mutual learning.

- Broadening Perspectives: Engaging with individuals from diverse backgrounds broadens one's worldview. Exposure to different ways of thinking and living enriches personal perspectives, contributing to a more well-rounded and informed understanding of the world.

- Fostering Creativity and Innovation: Diverse perspectives stimulate creativity and innovation. In relationships, the interplay of varied ideas and approaches can lead to innovative solutions, fostering a dynamic and adaptive environment.

- Enhancing Problem-Solving Skills: Interacting with diverse individuals encourages the development of efficient problem-solving skills. The ability to navigate different viewpoints promotes collaborative solutions to challenges.

- Promoting Inclusivity: Appreciating diversity creates inclusive environments where individuals feel valued and accepted for who they are. This inclusivity strengthens connections by fostering a sense of belonging and shared respect.

Navigating Differences:
While diversity enriches relationships, navigating differences requires intentional effort and effective communication. Strategies for navigating differences include:

- Active Listening: Actively listen to understand the perspectives of others. Individuals contribute to a more inclusive and understanding environment by genuinely hearing and acknowledging different viewpoints.

- Cultivating Empathy: Cultivate empathy to understand the emotions and experiences of those with differing viewpoints. Empathy builds bridges of understanding and fosters a connection despite differences.

- Seeking Common Ground: Identify common values, goals, or interests that can serve as a foundation for connection. Finding shared ground can create a sense of unity and help navigate differences more constructively.

- Polite Dialogue: Engage in open and polite dialogue. Create an environment where individuals feel comfortable expressing their views without fear of judgment, encouraging a healthy exchange of ideas.

- Cultural Competence: Develop cultural competence by educating oneself about different cultures and perspectives. This awareness enhances understanding and minimizes misunderstandings based on cultural differences.

- Collaborative Problem-Solving: Approach conflicts or challenges collaboratively. By working together to find solutions, individuals can leverage the strengths of diverse perspectives, leading to more effective problem-solving.

- Flexibility and Adaptability: Embrace flexibility and adaptability in navigating differences. Recognize that diversity is not static, and being open to adapting one's perspectives contributes to harmonious relationships.

- Conflict Resolution Skills: Develop efficient conflict resolution skills. Addressing conflicts effectively involves finding common ground, understanding the root causes, and working towards mutually beneficial solutions.

- Promoting Inclusive Language: Use language that promotes inclusivity and avoids assumptions or stereotypes. Inclusive communication fosters an environment where diverse perspectives are welcomed and respected.

- Building Mutual Trust: Trust is essential in navigating differences. Building and maintaining trust involves consistent and transparent communication, demonstrating reliability, and valuing the perspectives of others.

Individuals contribute to more inclusive, respectful, and harmonious relationships by appreciating diversity and implementing effective strategies to navigate differences. These efforts enrich personal connections and contribute to a more tolerant and understanding society.

- **The Art of Forgiveness and Repairing Bonds**

Understanding Forgiveness:
Forgiveness is a transformative process that holds the power to mend strained relationships and promote healing. Exploring its nature within the context of relationships reveals its profound impact.

- Emotional Liberation: Forgiveness liberates individuals from the emotional burdens of resentment, anger, and hurt. By letting go of negative emotions, individuals experience a sense of emotional freedom, contributing to their well-being.

- Rebuilding Trust: Forgiveness is a crucial step in rebuilding trust within relationships. It signals a willingness to move forward and rebuild, creating a foundation for renewed trust and acceptance.

- Promoting Empathy: The act of forgiveness often involves empathizing with the perspectives and experiences of others. This empathetic acceptance fosters a deeper connection and a more compassionate approach to resolving conflicts.

- Breaking the Cycle of Resentment: Forgiveness interrupts the cycle of resentment and retaliation, allowing for a fresh start. It is an opportunity to break free from negative patterns and create a more positive and constructive relational dynamic.

- Facilitating Personal Growth: Forgiveness contributes to personal growth by encouraging individuals to reflect on their behaviours and responses. It promotes self-awareness and resilience, fostering individual development within the relationship.

Practical Steps for Repair

Navigating conflicts, fostering forgiveness, and rebuilding trust requires intentional and actionable steps. Here are practical strategies to guide this process:

Open Communication:
   - Create a Safe Space: Establish an environment where both parties feel comfortable expressing their thoughts and emotions without fear of judgment.
   - Active Listening: Practice Active listening to ensure everyone feels heard and understood.

Express Feelings and Perspectives:
   - Share Emotions: Encourage open expression of feelings and perspectives. It creates an opportunity for understanding the root causes of the conflict.
   - Use "I" Statements: Frame discussions using "I" statements to express personal feelings and experiences, minimizing blame and defensiveness.

Seek Acceptance:
   - Empathize: Put yourself in the other person's shoes to better understand their point of view.
   - Clarify Misunderstandings: Address any misunderstandings or misinterpretations that may have contributed to the conflict.

Apologize and Accept Responsibility:

- Sincere Apology: If applicable, offer a sincere apology for any actions or words that may have caused harm.
- Accept Responsibility: Take ownership of mistakes and demonstrate commitment to positive change.

Establish Boundaries:
- Set Clear Expectations: Define clear boundaries and expectations moving forward to avert recurring conflicts.
- Mutual Agreement: Ensure that both parties agree on the terms for rebuilding trust and moving forward.

Commit to Change:
- Identify Areas for Improvement: Reflect on areas for personal growth and improvement within the relationship.
- Develop Action Plans: Collaboratively create action plans to address specific issues and prevent future conflicts.

Counselling or Mediation:
- Professional Guidance: Seek the assistance of a neutral third party, such as a counsellor or mediator, to facilitate communication and resolution.

- Objective Perspective: A professional can provide an objective perspective and guide the process toward constructive outcomes.

Time and Patience:
  - Recognize Healing Takes Time: Understand that forgiveness and rebuilding trust take time. Be patient and allow the process of healing to unfold naturally.
  - Consistent Effort: Consistently demonstrate commitment to positive change through ongoing efforts and actions.

Celebrate Progress:
  - Acknowledge Positive Steps: Celebrate small victories and positive changes in the relationship.
  - Express Appreciation: Express gratitude for the efforts made by both parties to repair and strengthen the relationship.

Rebuilding Shared Positive Experiences:
  - Create New Memories: Engage in activities that foster positive experiences and shared memories.
  - Focus on Connection: Shift the focus toward rebuilding the connection and fostering mutual enjoyment.

By integrating these practical steps into the process of repairing strained relationships, individuals can navigate conflicts, foster forgiveness, and gradually rebuild trust. The key lies in maintaining open communication, empathy, and a commitment to positive change, laying the groundwork for healthier and more resilient connections.

• Shared Goals and Meaningful Connections

Aligning Values:
Alignment of values and goals is necessary in fostering deeper connections within relationships. Understanding the significance of shared values contributes to the richness and longevity of connections.

- Foundation of Connection: Shared values is a solid foundation for connection. When individuals have the same beliefs, principles, and priorities, it creates a sense of alignment and unity within the relationship.

- Mutual Understanding: Shared values facilitate mutual understanding between individuals. It allows them to navigate challenges with a similar perspective, fostering a deep connection rooted in a shared understanding of what is necessary.

- Enhanced Communication: Alignment of values contributes to enhanced communication. Individuals with shared values often find it easier to express themselves openly and feel confident that their viewpoints are understood and respected.

- Cohesive Decision-Making: Aligning values in relationships, whether personal or professional promotes cohesive decision-making. Individuals can collaboratively make choices that resonate with their shared principles, creating a harmonious and cooperative environment.

- Strengthening Resilience: Shared values contribute to the resilience of relationships. During challenging times, a shared value system provides a framework for individuals to support each other and work together to overcome obstacles.

- Creating a Shared Vision: Aligning values allows individuals to create a shared vision for the future. This shared vision becomes a guiding force that inspires joint efforts, collaboration, and the pursuit of common goals.

Collaborative Growth:
Collaborative growth within a relationship involves supporting each other's personal development and aspirations. This dynamic process contributes to the overall health and fulfillment within the relationship.

- Encouraging Individual Aspirations: In a supportive relationship, individuals are encouraged to pursue their aspirations and goals. This encouragement fosters a sense of autonomy and empowerment.

- Shared Learning Experiences: Collaborative growth involves sharing learning experiences. Individuals within the relationship become partners in each other's journeys, providing insights, encouragement, and constructive feedback.

- Mutual Inspiration: Supporting personal growth creates an environment where individuals inspire each other. Witnessing and contributing to the other person's achievements is motivating and uplifting, strengthening the emotional connection.

- Adapting Together: Collaborative growth requires adaptability. Individuals learn to adapt to each other's evolving goals, preferences, and aspirations, creating a dynamic and flexible relationship.

- Celebrating Achievements: Acknowledging and celebrating each other's achievements is necessary for collaborative growth. This celebration reinforces a positive and supportive atmosphere within the relationship.

- Fostering a Growth Mindset: Collaborative growth is rooted in a growth mindset, where individuals view challenges as opportunities for learning and development. This mindset contributes to resilience and adaptability within the relationship.

- Balancing Individual and Shared Goals: Striking a balance between individual and shared goals is essential for collaborative growth. It involves open communication, negotiation, and a shared commitment to personal fulfillment and collective aspirations.

- Creating a Supportive Environment: A relationship that values collaborative growth provides a supportive environment for each individual to explore, experiment, and evolve. This support contributes to a sense of security and trust within the partnership.

- Building a Shared Future: Collaborative growth ultimately involves building a shared future. Individuals within the relationship actively contribute to each other's journeys, creating a collective narrative encompassing shared experiences and aspirations.

• **Nurturing Connection in the Digital Age**

Balancing Digital and Face-to-Face Connections:

The impact of technology on relationships is significant, shaping how individuals connect and communicate. Maintaining a balance between digital and face-to-face interactions is crucial for fostering genuine connections in the digital age:

- Advantages of Digital Connections:
  - Accessibility: Technology enables instant communication, making it easier to stay connected regardless of geographical distances.
  - Efficiency: Digital platforms facilitate quick and efficient information exchange, enhancing communication in various aspects of life.

- Challenges of Excessive Digital Engagement:
  - Superficial Connections: Overreliance on digital communication may result in superficial connections, lacking the depth of in-person interactions.
  - Misinterpretation: Digital communication may lead to misinterpretation, as non-verbal cues are often absent, potentially causing misunderstandings.

- Strategies for Maintaining Genuine Connections:
  - Scheduled Face-to-Face Time: Prioritize regular in-person interactions to strengthen emotional bonds and foster deeper connections.

- Meaningful Digital Engagement: Use digital platforms intentionally, focusing on meaningful conversations rather than superficial exchanges.

- Balanced Communication Channels: Combine digital communication with traditional methods to ensure a well-rounded approach to staying connected.

- Shared Experiences: Engage in activities together, either in-person or virtually, to create shared experiences that contribute to a stronger connection.

- Active Listening Online: Practice active listening even in digital interactions, showing genuine interest and understanding.

Mindful Tech Use:
Maintaining a balance between online interactions and meaningful in-person connections involves adopting a mindful approach to technology use:

- Set Boundaries:
  - Establish Tech-Free Zones: Designate specific times or places as tech-free, allowing undistracted face-to-face interactions.
  - Define Screen Time Limits: Set limits on screen time to avoid excessive digital engagement and prioritize in-person connections.

- Prioritize Quality Over Quantity:

- Meaningful Digital Interactions: Focus on meaningful conversations online rather than excessive, superficial exchanges.
- Quality Face-to-Face Time: When meeting in person, prioritize quality time over quantity, fostering deep connections.

- Be Present in Person and Online:
  - Limit Multitasking: Avoid multitasking while engaging digitally or in person to ensure total presence and attention.
  - Mindful Use of Devices: Use devices mindfully, avoiding distractions during face-to-face interactions to enhance connection.

- Use Technology to Enhance, Not Replace:
  - Augmenting, Not Replacing: Use technology to enhance connections, supplementing rather than replacing face-to-face interactions.
  - Share Experiences Virtually: Use online platforms to share experiences, photos, or updates, providing a virtual window into each other's lives.

- Prioritize In-Person Celebrations:
  - Celebrate Milestones Face-to-Face: Reserve significant celebrations and milestones for in-person gatherings to strengthen emotional bonds.

- Digital Supplements: While digital celebrations have their place, prioritize in-person connections for relevant life events.

- Practice Digital Detox:
  - Scheduled Breaks: Implement scheduled digital detox periods to disconnect and focus on in-person relationships.
  - Nature of Connection: Remind yourself of the unique value of face-to-face connections and the emotional depth they provide.

- Regularly Assess and Adjust:
  - Reflection on Tech Use: Periodically reflect on your technology use and its impact on your relationships.
  - Adjust Habits Accordingly: Adjust your tech habits to ensure a healthy balance between digital and face-to-face connections.

By consciously balancing digital and face-to-face interactions and adopting mindful tech use, individuals can navigate the challenges of the digital age while nurturing genuine and meaningful connections in both virtual and physical realms.

- **The Role of Rituals and Traditions**

Creating Meaningful Rituals:
Rituals and traditions play a vital role in deepening connections within relationships. They provide a sense of continuity, shared history, and emotional resonance.

- Establishing Routine and Predictability:
  - Emotional Stability: Rituals create a sense of emotional stability and predictability within relationships, offering comfort and reassurance.
  - Bonding Through Routine: Participating in regular rituals fosters a shared routine, contributing to a sense of togetherness and commitment.

- Symbolic Expression of Connection:
  - Shared Symbolism: Rituals often involve symbolic actions or gestures that express shared meanings and reinforce the connection between individuals.
  - Shared Identity: Through participation in rituals, individuals establish a shared identity within the relationship, strengthening their sense of belonging.

- Celebrating Milestones and Achievements:
  - Marking Important Moments: Rituals provide a structured way to celebrate milestones, achievements, and special occasions, turning them into memorable and significant events.

- Reflecting on Growth: Regularly engaging in rituals allows individuals to reflect on personal and relational growth, creating a narrative of shared experiences.

- Building Emotional Intimacy:
  - Emotional Connection: Rituals often involve moments of emotional intimacy, allowing individuals to express vulnerability and deepen their emotional connection.
  - Shared Rituals, Shared Emotions: Engaging in mutual activities fosters a sense of shared emotional experiences, contributing to a stronger bond.

Adapting and Creating New Traditions:
The adaptability and creation of traditions are essential in maintaining the relevance and vibrancy of connections within relationships.

- Changing Dynamics and Evolving Relationships:
  - Flexibility in Traditions: Recognize that traditions can be changed to accommodate changing dynamics as relationships evolve.
  - Reflecting Current Realities: Adapting traditions ensures they remain reflective of current realities and aspirations of those involved.

Fostering a Sense of Renewal:

- New Beginnings: Creating new traditions allows a sense of renewal within the relationship, bringing excitement and anticipation.
- Shared Ownership: Individuals actively participating in new traditions feel a sense of ownership, reinforcing their commitment to the relationship.

- Tailoring Traditions to Individuals:
  - Personalization: Adapting traditions to suit individual preferences ensures they resonate personally, enhancing their meaningfulness.
  - Inclusivity: Creating new traditions provides an opportunity to include diverse perspectives and preferences, fostering inclusivity within the relationship.

- Celebrating Growth and Change:
  - Reflecting Relationship Development: Adapting traditions can symbolize the growth and evolution of the relationship over time.
  - Embracing Change: Creating new traditions allows individuals to embrace change and approach the future with excitement and optimism.

- Connecting Generations and Shared Values:

- Passing Down Traditions: Established traditions often involve passing down values and practices through generations. Adapting and creating new traditions allows for the incorporation of contemporary values.
- Reflecting Shared Values: New traditions can be incorporated to reflect shared values and aspirations of individuals within the relationship, ensuring relevance and resonance.

- Building Anticipation and Excitement:
  - Anticipation for New Experiences: Adoption of new traditions builds anticipation for shared experiences, contributing to a sense of excitement within the relationship.
  - Dynamic and Ever-Changing: A willingness to create new traditions keeps the relationship dynamic and ever-changing, fostering continual growth and exploration.

Meaningful rituals and adaptable traditions contribute to the depth and vibrancy of connections within relationships. By engaging in established rituals and being open to adapting or creating new traditions, individuals actively participate in the ongoing narrative of their relationship, creating a rich tapestry of shared experiences, emotions, and growth.

- **Reciprocity and Shared Responsibility**

Mutual Contribution:
Reciprocity, or mutual contribution, is fundamental to maintaining balanced and fulfilling relationships. It involves a give-and-take dynamic that fosters a sense of equity, shared responsibility, and interdependence.

Foundation of Trust:
  - Trust Through Reciprocity: Reciprocal actions build trust within relationships. When individuals contribute mutually, it creates a foundation of trust and reliability.
  - Balanced Interactions: A sense of balance in giving and receiving fosters a healthy and equitable relationship dynamic.

Emotional Connection:
  - Emotional Support: Reciprocity in emotional support strengthens the emotional connection between individuals. Being there for each other in times of need creates a sense of security.
  - Shared Vulnerability: When both parties contribute emotionally, it establishes a shared vulnerability that deepens understanding and empathy.

Building a Partnership:
  - Collaborative Decision-Making: Mutual contribution extends to collaborative decision-making. Shared

responsibilities in decision-making create a partnership based on equality.

- Joint Planning: Planning and navigating life together involve both individuals actively participating, ensuring a sense of shared responsibility for the relationship's direction.

Balancing Efforts:

- Equitable Efforts: Reciprocity involves balance in effort and investment from both parties. When both individuals contribute equally, it prevents feelings of imbalance or resentment.
- Respecting Individual Capacities: Recognizing and respecting each other's capacities and limitations ensures that contributions align with realistic expectations.

Promoting Personal Growth:

- Encouraging Growth: Mutual contribution supports personal growth for both individuals. Each person's contribution becomes an opportunity for learning, development, and mutual empowerment.
- Creating a Supportive Environment: A relationship where both individuals contribute to each other's growth fosters an environment of encouragement and motivation.

Shared Responsibility for Connection:

Maintaining the health and vitality of connections involves a collective effort from both individuals. Shared responsibility for connection is crucial for nurturing and sustaining meaningful relationships.

Effective Communication:
 - Open Dialogue: Both individuals contribute to open communication. Actively expressing thoughts, feelings, and concerns ensures transparency and understanding.
 - Active Listening: Listening with empathy and attention is a shared responsibility that enhances communication and strengthens connection.

Resolving Conflicts Together:
 - Collaborative Conflict Resolution: When conflicts arise, individuals resolve issues collaboratively. Shared responsibility for conflict resolution promotes understanding and compromise.
 - Learning and Growing from Challenges: Facing challenges together and learning from them is a joint effort that contributes to the resilience of the relationship.

Quality Time and Presence:
 - Shared Commitment to Quality Time: Spending meaningful time together requires a joint commitment. Prioritizing quality moments builds intimacy and connection.

- Being Present: Both individuals contribute to being present in the moment, minimizing distractions and enhancing the depth of shared experiences.

Expressing Appreciation:
  - Mutual Gratitude: Expressing appreciation for each other's contributions is a shared responsibility. Recognizing and acknowledging efforts strengthen the sense of value within the relationship.
  - Reciprocal Affection: Both individuals contribute to expressing affection, ensuring a mutual and balanced exchange of love and care.

Setting and Achieving Goals:
  - Joint Goal-Setting: Setting and working towards common goals involves shared responsibility. Collaborative goal-setting fosters a sense of unity and purpose.
  - Supporting Individual Aspirations: While working on shared goals, individuals also support each other's aspirations, creating a holistic approach to personal and shared achievements.

Celebrating Successes Together:
  - Shared Joy in Achievements: Celebrating successes together is a shared responsibility that enhances the joy of accomplishments. Shared happiness strengthens the bond between individuals.

- Encouraging Each Other: Contributing to each other's successes involves providing encouragement and support, creating a sense of shared achievement.

Reciprocity in relationships forms the bedrock of trust and balance, while shared responsibility for connection ensures that both individuals actively contribute to the health and vitality of their relationship. By fostering mutual contribution and embracing shared responsibility, individuals create a resilient and fulfilling partnership that stands the test of time.

- **Reflecting on Connection as a Lifelong Journey**

Continuous Growth:
Emphasizing that connections evolve and require ongoing effort is crucial for sustaining fulfilling relationships. Continuous growth involves a dynamic and intentional approach to building connections:

Embracing Change:
  - Natural Evolution: Recognize that relationships naturally evolve and undergo changes. Embracing this evolution allows individuals to adapt to new phases and dynamics.

- Opportunities for Growth: Viewing change as an opportunity for growth within the relationship fosters a positive and proactive mindset.

- Lifelong Learning:
  - Understanding Each Other: Continuous growth involves ongoing efforts to understand and learn about each other. Individuals evolve, and staying attuned to these changes promotes a deeper connection.
  - Curiosity and Exploration: Cultivating curiosity about each other's evolving interests, goals, and perspectives encourages continual exploration and learning.

- Adapting Communication Styles:
  - Communication Evolution: Recognize that communication styles may evolve. Adaptability to changes ensures that individuals remain connected through effective and evolving communication.
  - Open Dialogue About Changes: Encouraging open dialogue about evolving communication preferences allows for mutual understanding and adjustment.

Navigating Life Transitions:
  - Supporting Each Other Through Transitions: Life transitions impact relationships. Continuous growth involves supporting each other through transitions, whether they be personal or professional.

- Adaptability During Changes: Adapting to new roles, responsibilities, or circumstances requires flexibility and a collaborative approach to maintain connection.

Shared Experiences:
  - Creating New Memories: Creating new shared experiences becomes essential as connections evolve. Continually seeking out opportunities to build memories together strengthens the fabric of the relationship.
  - Reflecting on the Journey: Regularly reflecting on the journey of the relationship allows individuals to appreciate the shared history and envision the path forward.

Reflection and Adaptation:
Reflecting on connections, adapting to changing dynamics, and investing in the continual nourishment of relationships is a proactive approach to sustaining and enhancing connections.

Regular Self-Reflection:
  - Personal Growth and Contribution: Individuals should self-reflect to identify areas for personal growth within the relationship and assess their contributions.

- Assessment of Needs: Regularly reflecting on individual needs and desires in the relationship enables better communication and understanding.

Mutual Reflection:
  - Joint Assessment: Encouraging mutual reflection involves both individuals assessing the health and satisfaction of the relationship. Open conversations about aspirations, concerns, and expectations contribute to shared growth.
  - Feedback and Communication: Offering constructive feedback and actively listening to each other's reflections fosters a culture of continuous improvement.

Adaptability and Flexibility:
  - Embracing Change Together: Couples should approach change as a shared journey. Mutual adaptability and flexibility ensure that both individuals contribute to navigating transitions successfully.
  - Joint Decision-Making: In times of change, involving both parties in decision-making promotes collaboration and shared responsibility.

Investing in Relationship Skills:
  - Communication Enhancement: Recognizing the need for ongoing improvement in communication skills is essential. Investing time and effort in

enhancing communication fosters a deeper connection.

- Learning and Growing Together: Actively seeking resources and information to strengthen relationship skills ensures that individuals grow together, continually enriching their connection.

Celebrate Milestones and Achievements:

- Acknowledging Progress: Reflecting on shared milestones and achievements provides an opportunity for celebration and reinforcement of the positive aspects of the relationship.

- Setting New Goals: After reflection, setting new goals together ensures a shared vision for the future and a commitment to ongoing growth.

Prioritizing Quality Time:

- Regular Assessments: Evaluating the quality of time spent together allows individuals to identify areas for improvement and enhance the overall experience of connection.

- Adapting Activities: Adapting shared activities and finding new ways to spend meaningful time together contributes to ongoing satisfaction.

This chapter has served as a compass for navigating the profound waters of connection. By exploring the layers of connection, embracing vulnerability, cultivating emotional intelligence, bridging differences, forgiving and repairing bonds, aligning values, navigating the digital landscape, embracing rituals, understanding reciprocity, and reflecting on the lifelong journey of connection, readers will unlock the potential for more fulfilling relationships that stand the test of time.

Chapter Seven

Tools for Stormy Seas: Navigating Difficult Personalities - Turning Discord into Opportunities for Growth

In the intricate dance of relationships, encounters with difficult personalities are inevitable. Rather than viewing these challenges as insurmountable obstacles, this chapter delves into practical tools and strategies to navigate stormy seas, transforming conflicts into opportunities for personal and relational growth.

Understanding Difficult Personalities
• Empathy as a Compass:
   - Cultivate empathy as a guiding force when dealing with difficult personalities. Understanding their perspectives fosters a connection and opens avenues for constructive communication.

• Identifying Triggers:
   - Uncover the triggers that contribute to challenging behaviours. Identifying these triggers allows for a proactive approach to managing and defusing potential conflicts.

• Maintaining Emotional Regulation:

- Equip yourself with emotional regulation techniques. By staying composed in the face of challenging interactions, you create a foundation for productive dialogue.

Strategies for Effective Communication
- Active Listening Amidst Discord:
   - Implement active listening even in challenging conversations. By actively hearing the concerns of difficult personalities, you pave the way for mutual understanding.

- Calm and Assertive Communication:
   - Adopt a calm and assertive communication style. This approach fosters respect and prevents escalation, creating a space for constructive dialogue.

- Choosing Battles Wisely:
   - Learn to discern between battles worth fighting and those better left untouched. Strategic choices in addressing conflicts contribute to a more harmonious relationship.

Turning Discord into Opportunities for Growth
- Constructive Feedback and Boundary Setting:
   - Provide constructive feedback while setting clear boundaries. Establishing expectations and

communicating them contributes to a healthier dynamic.

• Encouraging Personal Reflection:
   - Encourage personal reflection. Foster an environment where difficult personalities can reflect on their behaviour, promoting individual growth.

Personal and Relational Growth
• Learning from Challenges:
   - View challenges as learning opportunities. Embracing difficulties as a pathway to growth shifts the narrative from conflicts to a shared journey of personal and relational development.

• Adapting to Diversity:
   - Embrace diversity in personalities. Recognizing and valuing differences contribute to a more inclusive and understanding relationship.

• Leveraging Conflict for Positive Change:
   - Transform conflict into a catalyst for positive change. Use conflicts as a platform to address underlying issues and collaboratively work towards solutions.

Navigating difficult personalities is an inherent part of the relational landscape. By employing these tools for stormy seas, individuals can transform challenging interactions into opportunities for personal and mutual growth. This chapter serves as a guide to weathering the storms and emerging from them with strengthened connections and a deeper understanding of oneself and others.

Chapter Eight

Companion on the Journey - Beyond a Guide: Your Companion to Becoming a Masterful Communicator

In the grand tapestry of human connection, communication is the loom weaving the threads of understanding and intimacy. This chapter transcends the role of a guide, positioning itself as your devoted companion to becoming a masterful communicator.

The Essence of Masterful Communication

- **Authenticity as the North Star**
  - Embrace authenticity as the guiding principle of masterful communication. Being true to oneself forms the foundation for genuine and meaningful exchanges.

- **Curiosity as a Driving Force**
  - Cultivate an insatiable curiosity. The quest to understand others fuels the desire to explore diverse perspectives, enriching the tapestry of communication.

Nurturing the Art of Listening
- Deep Listening Techniques:

- Explore deep listening techniques. Beyond hearing words, masterful communication involves attuning to nuances, emotions, and the unspoken layers beneath the surface.

• **Empathetic Understanding**
  - Develop empathetic understanding. Masterful communicators grasp the content of messages and empathize with the emotions and experiences conveyed.

The Dance of Verbal Expression

• **Clarity and Precision in Expression:**
  - Hone clarity and precision in verbal expression. Masterful communicators articulate thoughts with eloquence, ensuring their messages are accurately received.

• **Adapting Communication Styles:**
  - Learn the art of adapting communication styles. Tailoring your approach to different individuals and contexts enhances the effectiveness of your messages.

Navigating Non-Verbal Realms

• Mastering Body Language:

- Delve into the intricacies of body language. Understanding and harnessing non-verbal cues enriches the depth and subtlety of your communicative prowess.

• The Harmony of Tone and Pitch:
  - Appreciate the nuances of tone and pitch. Masterful communicators wield these elements like a maestro, orchestrating a symphony that resonates with their audience.

Beyond Words: Emotional Intelligence

• Cultivating Emotional Intelligence:
  - Elevate your communication through emotional intelligence. Recognizing and managing emotions, both yours and others, enhances the empathetic and insightful dimensions of conversations.

• Responding, Not Reacting:
  - Practice responsive communication. Instead of reactive responses, masterful communicators take a moment to consider and respond thoughtfully, fostering deep connections.

Your Continuous Journey

- Lifelong Learning in Communication:
   - Embrace communication as a lifelong learning journey. A masterful communicator remains open to evolving strategies, embracing new insights, and refining their skills.

- Cultivating Connection as a Lifestyle:
   - Integrate masterful communication into your lifestyle. Transform communication from a skill set into a way of being, fostering enduring connections in all facets of life.

The Journey's End is a New Beginning

Remember that the journey to becoming a masterful communicator is not a destination but a continuous exploration. Your companion on this path extends beyond these pages, urging you to embark on a lifelong adventure, discovering the boundless possibilities of connection through the artistry of communication.

Conclusion

Navigating Life's Waters with The Communication Compass

In the vast expanse of human experience, the art of communication emerges as the guiding star that illuminates our journey, shaping the contours of our relationships and navigating the seas of connection. As we bid farewell to the pages of "The Communication Compass: Guiding Lights for Building Rapport, Trust, and Fulfilling Connections," let us reflect on the profound odyssey we've undertaken together.

A Tapestry Woven with Understanding
Through the chapters of this book, we have unravelled the intricacies of communication, exploring its multifaceted dimensions as a compass guiding us through the realms of rapport, trust, and profound connections. The threads of authenticity, empathy, and curiosity have woven a tapestry rich with insights and actionable tools, offering a roadmap for transformative communication.

From Guide to Companion
This journey transcends the conventional role of a guide; it extends an invitation to embrace this book

as a lifelong companion. The principles shared within these pages are not mere directives but loyal companions on your voyage toward becoming a masterful communicator. Together, we've navigated stormy seas, adapted to changing tides, and discovered the beauty of continuous growth in our connections.

The Dance of Understanding and Expression

Within the dance of communication, we've explored the symphony of words and the subtleties of non-verbal cues. We've championed the causes of deep listening and empathetic understanding, recognizing the transformative power of clarity and precision in our expressions. The harmony of tone, pitch, and body language has become our guide in orchestrating connections that resonate with authenticity and depth.

Embracing Emotional Intelligence

As we conclude this voyage, the call to cultivate emotional intelligence echoes profoundly. Responding thoughtfully, not reacting impulsively, becomes the compass that steers us towards more meaningful interactions. This conclusion is not an endpoint but a launching pad for a new beginning—an invitation to integrate masterful communication into the very fabric of our lives.

A Lifelong Adventure

The title "The Communication Compass" extends beyond its literal meaning; it encapsulates the spirit of a journey—an adventure that transcends the boundaries of words. Let this compass be your steadfast companion as you embark on the endless voyage of lifelong learning, adapting, and cultivating connections as a way of life.

In Gratitude and Connection

As you close this book, let gratitude be the wind that fills your sails. Gratitude for the moments of insight, the challenges that fostered growth, and the connections you've nurtured. May The Communication Compass continue to be your companion, pointing you towards authentic connections and guiding lights illuminating the path to fulfilling relationships.

Fair winds and following seas on your ongoing odyssey of communication mastery. May your connections be profound, your trust unwavering, and your rapport an enduring testament to the artistry of genuine communication. Until we meet again on the shores of understanding, keep navigating with intention, empathy, and the joy of truly connecting.

www.ingramcontent.com/pod-product-compliance
Lightning Source LLC
Chambersburg PA
CBHW071054240526
45471CB00015B/1882